# POWER
## THE SUCCESS MANTRA

**SECRETS TO CREATING BUSINESS SUCCESS**

BY
VIKRANT SHAURYA

PUBLISHED BY

P.O.W.E.R by Vikrant Shaurya

Published by
**Authority on Demand**

ISBN-13: 978-1976557484
ISBN-10: 1976557488

No part of this book may be reproduced or utilized in any form or by any means, electronic or mechanical including photocopying, recording or by any information storage and retrieval system, without permission in writing from the publisher.

www.AuthorityOnDemand.com

© 2017 Vikrant Shaurya

I dedicate this book, with deep respect and great love, to my parents. You gave me not only the gift of life but also an unrelenting passion to live it fully. For that, I'm so very grateful.

# TABLE OF CONTENTS

| | |
|---|---|
| Preface | 11 |
| Who Am I? | 13 |
| Prologue | 17 |
| P.O.W.E.R. - The Success Mantra | 21 |
| Passion | 25 |

How do you find your ultimate bliss? 35

What's the simplest way to choose your profession? 37

How can passion generate new opportunities for you? 39

How can you become an energy power-house? 41

How can you find your vision through your Passion? 43

How does passion influence the people around you? 45

| | |
|---|---|
| Optimism | 51 |

How can you turn a business problem into an opportunity? 57

How can you persuade people for good? 59

How can you develop a never quit, no matter what attitude? 61

How can you help people evolve? 63

How can you be optimistic and be unimaginably happy? 66

| WILLPOWER | 72 |
|---|---|
| How can you attain self-discipline and achieve whatever you desire in your life? | 75 |
| Actionable Exercises for you to Develop Willpower in an easy way: | 78 |
| How to be the boss of your own mind! | 80 |
| How to be what you desire to be. | 84 |

| ENDURANCE | 88 |
|---|---|
| What trait should you develop for never losing in life? | 92 |
| What Endurance can do for you? | 94 |
| Which fights are worth fighting? | 96 |
| How to endure and stay strong in your life | 98 |
| How to stand against all odds | 100 |
| What does the Bible say about endurance? | 103 |
| How Gandhi defeated the British | 105 |

| RATIONALE | 109 |
|---|---|
| How not to be like Hitler | 116 |
| What is the 7-step guide to rational decision making? | 119 |
| What do you need to stay in the game for the long term? | 122 |
| How can you manage your team so that they can trust you? | 124 |

| | |
|---|---|
| **Nucleus of the P.O.W.E.R. Star: Vision** | **132** |
| How to create your vision in 4 simple steps? | 138 |
| Why do you need to start with a vision? | 140 |
| How can you use the law of attraction to fuel your vision? | 142 |
| What happens if you go on without a vision? | 145 |
| Why would you fail in life? | 148 |
| How can you find your purpose instantly? | 151 |
| **THE SWAN SONG- The last-minute P.O.W.E.R.** | **155** |
| **IN A NUTSHELL** | **157** |
| **About the Author!** | **160** |

# **PREFACE**

Dear Readers,

Congratulations! You're now one step closer to realizing your dreams of living an enriching and meaningful life with a career that excites and challenges you and a personal life that you wouldn't trade away for anything in the World.

Before we get on with it, take a moment to imagine something with me. You wake up every day, not dreading going to work but actually looking forward to getting everything done. You leave your bed in full spirits and go to work excited to meet the challenges today. After work, you meet your friends and hangout with them, unwinding after a long day and recharging your mental energy. Once you get home, you spend time with your family and enjoy their company. You go to bed without any stress and fall asleep instantly. Doesn't that sound like the perfect day?

Getting that perfect day isn't that difficult. Many have done so in the past and many more will do so in the future. So how do YOU get there? The answer lies in the pages that follow.

I'm so grateful to all of you who make up the loyal community of readers with whom I'm connected. Thank you for investing your time, effort, and money into this book. Trust me, you won't regret it.

Also, to the ones who pass on this book to friends, relatives, and neighbours, I am so grateful. You're multiplying the impact of each book. To the ones who take their valuable time to review and critique the book, your feedback is what will make the subsequent editions of the book better.

Having said all that, let's now dive right in and learn what true P.O.W.E.R. in entrepreneurship means.

## **WHO AM I?**

I don't believe that I've introduced myself properly. My name is Vikrant Shaurya and I'm a twenty-four-year-old entrepreneur and book launch manager. I'll tell you the story of my journey in more detail as we go along through the book but let me give you some salient points before we begin.

First, I would like to thank you for your trust and investment in giving your business a new direction. I understand that there's a wealth of material out there and the sheer quantity of it all can get really overwhelming at times. However, I've tried to pack as much insight into this book as possible so that you can get to the core advice I have to give without having to go through a lot of clutter. The related stories from my life will help you see how those principles would apply to your day-to-day life and, eventually, the running of your business.

I promise you, after reading this book, you'll have tons of reasons to go on, follow your passion and be the ultimate best in what you desire to pursue.

P.O.W.E.R. is only going to give you the information that you need to attain massive success in your business and a number of opportunities in a short time.

In this book, I'll tell you about the 5 pillars of business organization that aided me in winning my employees' hearts while running a prominent and profitable business at the same time.

The insights that I'll be sharing with you today helped me to discover the ultimate keys to SUCCESS and transformed me into a totally different professional.

Oh yes, calling yourself a professional does feel good.

Here are some of things you'll be able to do if you follow the insights in this book.

- build a team for yourself and get what you desire.

- act as a BIG MAGNET and attract tons of opportunities to grow your business to its maximum potential.

- make tons of cash by managing your team in a simple yet elegant manner!

If you're still not convinced and want to know more about me, or just want to get in touch, please visit www.vikrantshaurya.com. I'd be more than happy to see you there!

Oh yes, calling yourself a professional does feel good :-)

Here are some of things I hope you would be able to do if you follow the insights in this book.

- You'll be able to build a team for yourself & get what you want.

- You'll be able to act as a BIG MAGNET and attract tons of opportunities to grow your business to the zenith.

- You'll be able to make tons of cash by managing your team in a simple yet elegant manner!

If you are still not convinced & want to know more about me, or just want to get in touch, please visit www.vikrantshaurya.com I would be more than happy to see you there!

# PROLOGUE

2006, Age Fourteen

*I walked into the room absolutely terrified. I saw new faces everywhere, people talking fluently to each other, none of them even noticing me for more than a few seconds. Someone looked at me and whispered something in the ear of the person standing next to him; they both snigger. I felt like turning and running back to my house and never coming out of my room ever again. It had begun.*

*I had always been shy and introverted and never talked to anyone except my family and a few of my closest friends. I had always done well in my studies, and my parents had thought that I'd eventually grow out of it, but when I entered seventh grade without much improvement, they decided it was time to take some drastic measures. A local community center helped people get over their fear of public speaking by making them interact with other people and give speeches. My parents enrolled me there, hoping that I'd get over my shyness and fear of speaking with enough practice.*

*On my first day, I was told that I would have to address every person in the room (about 50) from a podium as some sort of an initiation. I tried every excuse I could think of to get out of it, but, apparently, the organizers had heard all of them and didn't even consider them. I was pushed into a line leading to the stage and asked to introduce myself to a room full of strangers.*

*I was terrified. I paid close attention to what the people before me were saying so that I could copy them and get it over with The boy ahead of me gave his introduction.*

*"Hello, my name is Sam. I'm a student in the 7th grade, and when I grow up, I want to be an engineer."*

*Phew! That sounded simple enough. I was reassured. I could do this! There was even something resembling an encouraging applause throughout the room that boosted my morale. I quickly ran through what I wanted to say in my head, then I blurted it out almost as quickly.*

*"Hello, my name is Vikrant. I'm fourteen years old, and when I grow up, I want to be an entrepreneur."*

*I held my breath as I waited for the applause to ring out, signalling that I was free to go, but nothing happened for a few seconds. Then someone let out a snigger. In a few moments, the entire hall was laughing.*

*I was stupefied. What had I done wrong? Had I mispronounced entrepreneur? Or was my name funny. I was close to tears when an older member of the center, a high school student, pulled me aside with a strong hand on my shoulders.*

*I still clearly remember what he said to me next, and I believe that it has been one of the defining moments of my life.*

*"You did well, kid! Next time, say something like doctor or engineer. Business isn't a right thing to say."*

*You might be horrified at this suggestion today, but when I was growing up, this thinking was common. Business wasn't accorded the respect it deserved, and, more often than not, it was seen as a career for people who had never tasted academic success in their life. This was where my journey started.*

# POWER
## THE SUCCESS MANTRA

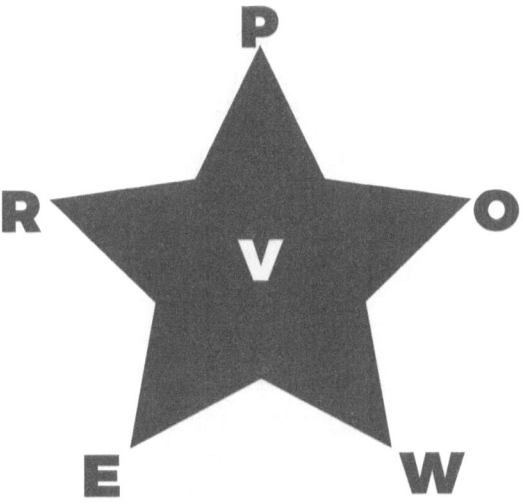

According to Keith Speights in a May, 2017 *USA Today* article, "Roughly 20% of new businesses survive past their first year of operation. That was the case two decades ago and is still the case today. However, around half of all businesses no longer exist after five years. Only one-third make it past their 10th anniversary. These statistics have been remarkably consistent through the years. Interestingly, major economic downturns don't seem to affect the survival rates for new businesses."

The word *success* has been tossed around so much these days that many people consider it to be a buzzword without much weight instead of fully appreciating what it represents. So, let's take a quick detour so that we can fully appreciate the power that the concept holds.

Most of the people whom you come across in your daily lives have a job in one way or another. They work for someone else, in someone else's company or organization and rarely do anything that lies outside the domain of their expertise. These employees, generally, need to be told what to do. Once they've been told what to do, which project to work on, which targets to achieve, they get to their job. But there's hardly any initiative in most of these people. This is why initiative and thinking outside the cubicle is so important today for anyone who desires to be successful.

Successful entrepreneurs go by many other names but there's one common thread that binds them all together. They are not just creative and innovative but also have the initiative to execute their brilliant ideas and work hard to give them value. Jing Zhou, coeditor of *The Oxford Handbook of Creativity, Innovation and Entrepreneurship,* said, "Research-based investigations of creativity, innovation and entrepreneurship have the potential to inform each other and enrich our knowledge of each of these areas... Yet, while these research streams have increasingly received a great deal of attention, they have developed largely independently of one another. The goal of our handbook is to address the critical need to integrate these three interrelated literatures."

What can you do to develop creativity, innovation, and entrepreneurship in yourself? This is where this book comes in. Over the course of my career, I've had some insights about the nature of entrepreneurship. I don't lay claim to them, of course. Many men and women, much more capable than I am, have talked about these principles but in different words. In this book, what I've achieved and can give to you, the reader, is a simple and easy way to chart your course as you progress toward your destination of becoming a successful entrepreneur.

Now, your path might be simple and mapping it might be easy, but walking it won't be easy. I'll talk about the most obvious pitfalls and problems that you might face on your path, but always remember that your journey is unique. You'll have to use your own discretion and best judgement to figure out a way that works for you. There will be situations when generic solutions won't work. You'll have to apply the principles in here to come to a solution that suits the situation you're in.

And after all, what good are entrepreneurs if they can't think on their own?

# PASSION

2009, Age Seventeen

*Hitler's propaganda director, Joseph Goebbels said, "If you tell a lie big enough and keep repeating it, people will eventually come to believe it." Something similar happened to me after that incident at the center.*

*Because of the community I grew up in and the way I was conditioned growing up, I managed to convince myself that I didn't desire to be an entrepreneur. I passed it off a childhood fantasy, like everyone scoffs at their childhood dreams of being an astronaut or a movie star once they grow up, and focused on my studies, determined to become an engineer.*

*I'd never had any experience with any form of engineering whatsoever. I had never built a thing in my life; I had no love for tools, no interest in coding, and no particular inclination toward math. I merely signed up for engineering because that was what all my friends were doing. I ditched my dreams and joined the rat race like a meek, middle-class child is supposed to. It's surprising how people have different metrics of success based upon how they grew up and what their economic status is. For someone from my social and economic class, academic success, a good college, a decently paying job was the pinnacle of human success and any other path to it was considered foolishness. However, if you look at any second generation entrepreneurs, you would hardly ever see them determining their worth as a function of their grades. This is a stark difference, and we'll deal with it later on at length. Now back to the story.*

*So, in my junior year, my father asked me what I wanted to do after high school. I mindlessly repeated what I had heard everyone else say and what was expected of me to say.*

*"I want to be an engineer."*

*However, this will be supported by anyone who has ever tried to do something they have no passion for, I failed miserably at it. I messed up my application process, my scores were bad, and I didn't get accepted into any college I had wanted to attend. I took a year off to work on my application, but the next year, I did just as bad.*

*Finally, because my father was convinced that I had a passion for engineering, he used his contacts and called in some other favors to somehow get me accepted into a college. I'm not sure how he did it, but I do know that he had to take out loans and sell some of his assets to get me in. This made the burden on me to succeed and do well to match up to his expectations much heavier.*

**"Whenever you find yourself on the side of the majority, it is time to pause and reflect." —Mark Twain**

Passion. You probably have heard this word a lot these days.

Somebody left their white-collar job to start a rather low-paying entrepreneurial venture.

Or somebody travelled miles and crossed two oceans to teach some impoverished people and children how to read and write.

Or a journalist risked his entire career just to protect the anonymity of a source.

Or a man with a camera stayed in threatening conditions in a foreign country that's in a constant state of anarchy and terrorism.

Do you ever wonder why these people do those things? Why do they take such risks when they could live their lives hassle-free, earning a six-figure salary in their 9-to-5 jobs?

They do it because of their passion for their own business, for writing, for teaching, for their belief in journalism, or for life in general.

Passion drives a human being to achieve what he or she is worthy of achieving.

You may stand unique among millions because of your passion. It may be anything you choose to pursue: your own business, singing, writing, reading, travelling, helping the poor, or any profession, for that matter. When you choose your passion as your profession, the work doesn't seem to be work at all; it becomes fun, enjoyable, and something you would do for free.

If you're passionate about anything, just about the time when you think you've lost, your passion emerges like a warrior and sets you back on the right track again.

Passion can also be associated with your profession. Working hard for something we don't care about leads to stress. Working hard for something we love is passion. People with stress want to retire as soon as possible and rightly so. But, people with a passion never retire.

So, whether we're thinking about starting a small business, or just thinking about what career path to choose, it's important that we follow our passions. When we think about what's needed to be successful in life and in our work, we usually think about characteristics like value, talent, ambition, intellect, discipline, persistence and luck. What many of us often fail to include in this recipe for success is passion. The passion we have, or don't have, for our work should not be underestimated. Sometimes, this ingredient could make the biggest difference of all.

Before we talk about what I mean by passion and why it's so important, we must first explore the true meaning of success. Success is usually assumed to be associated with large sums of wealth or a high level of fame, but true success isn't all about money.

Success is, or at least should be, primarily defined as an achievement of something desired.

So, the most successful people are the ones who achieve the things they most desire. What we desire the most, even more than money, is to be proud of what we do with our lives. This is especially true when it comes to our work. A truly successful person is one who is proud of the work he or she does. That is the true meaning of success.

Now, earning a lot of money shouldn't be the primary definition of success, but it's a reasonable goal to have. We all want to have enough money to sustain ourselves and our family. The thing is, if we're truly passionate about the work we do, there's probably a better than even chance that money will follow.

Passion is the powerful feeling of enthusiasm we all have inside us. We're all enthusiastic and passionate about something, whether it's finance, food, or a favorite sport. That enthusiasm is very powerful. When we can combine it with our work, we're setting ourselves up to achieving true success.

Ensuring that we're passionate about our work will provide us with not only a meaningful career but also a good chance of being paid well. The passion we have for our work can be the difference between merely surviving and thriving.

One of the most successful companies in the world today is Apple. When we think of Apple, we also think of Apple's first CEO, the late Steve Jobs. Carmine Gallo wrote an article in Forbes called, "The Seven Success Principles of Steve Jobs," which outlines seven key factors that were responsible for Jobs's success. The article is based on multiple interviews with Apple employees and Steve Jobs himself. Believe it or not, the No. 1 principle in this article is, "Do what you love." Steve Jobs believed in the power of passion and once said, "People with passion can change the world for the better." Jobs claimed that the passion he had for his work made all the difference.

These days, we cannot talk about success without mentioning Facebook and Facebook's CEO, Mark Zuckerberg. The thirty-two-year-old billionaire has changed the world we live in. David Kirkpatrick, in his book, The Facebook Effect: The inside Story of The Company That is Connecting the World, lists what he believes are Zuckerberg's ingredients for success. One of those ingredients is, you guessed it, follow your passion - not money. Zuckerberg suggests to "following your happiness," and explains that even if you don't end up making a fortune, you'll at least be doing what you love.

When you feel passionate about what you're doing, you'll radiate energy and enthusiasm. Others pick up on this, consciously or not, and are attracted to it. Passion is magnetic. Passion makes you set high goals. It gives you confidence and energy. Passion begets quality. When you're passionate, you don't want to stop halfway.

When you're passionate, you seek out what you desire. This is because you know what you desire. If you don't know what you desire, it's impossible to be passionate. But if you do know what you desire and are completely open with yourself, the urge to seek it will be irresistible. Indecision and uncertainty kills passion.

Good things come much more readily to those who are passionate. Passionate people seek out what they desire, but, in a way, they don't even have to. If you're passionate, if you know what you desire, you radiate an energy that brings your desires to you.

Passionate people excite others; they tend to make great first impressions. They make what they desire clear, explicitly or not, and people take notice. Others are often more than happy to help out the passionate: they may pull strings; they may collaborate; they may simply give their enthusiastic support. But they'll do something. Desiring something passionately produces circumstances that lead to getting it. A passionate person will get what she or he desires much more quickly and often than an indifferent person.

A "whole" life is one with parts that fit together. Such a life is devoid of contradictions; its elements don't compete with each other. Wholeness makes a person complete; it gives a person an identity and self-certainty that cannot be obtained otherwise. Though a passionate person may not lead a whole life, passion makes wholeness possible.

To live a whole life, you must know what you desire and seek it in all areas of your life. Wholeness allows the elements of life to work together, to aid one another. Wholeness brings a new level of meaning and purpose to your life beyond what passion can bring by itself.

What does "pursuing your passion" mean to you? People talk about it all the time, but what does it really mean? Does it mean quitting your day job and turning your love for crafts, photography, or food into your career?

My answer would be, maybe. It's very important for everyone to follow their passion and do what they feel inspired to do, but that may or may not mean turning it into a business. Maybe you like your day job, or you need the health benefits. If so, keep your job, but make sure you have some inspirational passion infused into your life as well.

No matter what you do in this life, one of the most fulfilling things you can do is follow your passion. Following your passion for work or for a hobby helps you tap into your gifts and talents. The act of following your passion allows you to gain skills in areas you're already strong in and pushes you to become better, which can then be shared with the world. In this way, you begin to create a body of work that will grow and develop over your lifetime. Keeping yourself engaged in meaningful work (hobbies apply here too) keeps your mind nimble as you age and allows you to feel that your life has great meaning and purpose.

Some people may not be ready to pursue their passion just

yet. If you're familiar with Maslow's hierarchy of needs, then you know that some basic needs must first be addressed before anyone can move forward with their passion. Those needs are having food, shelter, safety, love, friendship, and so forth. Once you have your basic needs met, then you're ready for self-actualization and some passion-following in your life.

Maslow's hierarchy of needs is depicted in the diagram below:

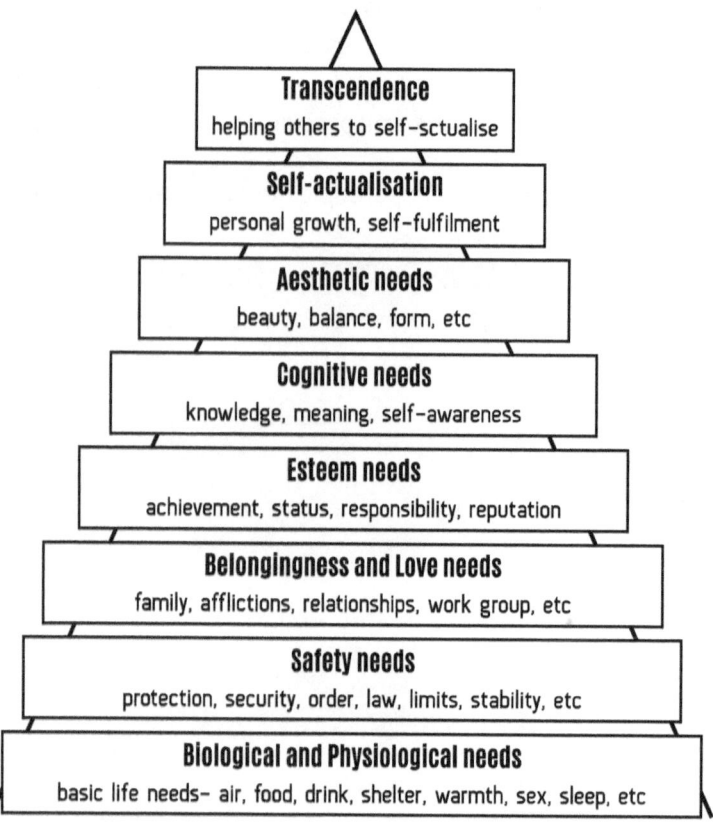

## HOW DO YOU FIND YOUR ULTIMATE BLISS?

Bliss can mean different things for different people. For some people, it might be having a secure job, where they get a paycheck at the start of every month and just have one set job to do. For others, it could mean running a business or a company. Everyone has a different and unique definition and idea of what their perfect life would be like. But sadly, very few people are able to get to their perfect life. Why?

The primary reason is that people don't stop and think about what they truly desire in their lives. They just follow the crowd and never stop to ask if what they're trying to accomplish is what they desire to do with their lives.

When you value your talents, devoting your time, energy, and resources to your passion, you'll experience some of the greatest bliss you could hope for. Some people have a passion in childhood that they give up on, like skateboarding, cross-stitching, or collecting vintage dresses. It's one thing to quit because you've lost your passion for it. It's another things to quit because it seems impractical. It's always practical to nurture and develop your passion, paid or unpaid, because it's tapping into your authentic self and growing that part of you.

The philosopher Alan Watts once gave a very simple test. He asked people to think of something that they would like to do if money were no object. He then asked them to do it anyway, insisting that the money would follow eventually.

It makes sense when you think about it. Once you're doing something you love, you can give it all your effort and energy, and your progress at it would be phenomenal. Soon enough, others will discover your talent and pay you to teach them, work for them, or give them products or services that they need from your areas of expertise.

Take a simple enough example. Pick something that you think is impractical and you can never make money out of. Let's say horseback riding. It's an expensive hobby, with no real practical usage in the modern day of cars and planes. But you really love riding horses. Then, I'd suggest that you stick with it. With time, you'll figure out a way to earn money from that. Maybe you could open a riding school, or act as a source of riders for movies or serials where they need horse-riders in large numbers; there are a lot of avenues. You only need to look for them hard enough. Once you do, you would be surprised to see that there's money to be made even from the most impractical and obsolete hobbies. The only criterion for your success is that you give it your all and always strive to be the best at it. Once you can do that, you'll pull it off!

## WHAT'S THE SIMPLEST WAY TO CHOOSE YOUR PROFESSION?

Profession's true meaning has been sadly lost over the course of the past few decades. It stems from an old Latin word *professio* that means 'to declare'. When you claim to be from a profession, you're essentially declaring that a particular skill is what you're an expert at. Now think about all the people you know in your daily life, who are working in jobs they hate. Are they really experts at what they do, or are they just trudging along, doing something they hate while magically hoping that their lives would change overnight, without really working toward that goal? Then, how can anyone expect to be an expert at something they hate doing? And if they're not an expert at it, would it really be their profession, or would it just be a job?

Choose something that you truly love doing. Then put in your time, effort, and resources into that one thing, bettering yourself every day at it. There's a rule that says that you need to put in 10,000 hours of practice into your skill to become a world class master it. You don't need to put in that much effort into something. If you can, that's well and good, but proficiency is much quicker to come by. If you take the time to pursue your passion, what you're essentially doing is developing your skills and gifts, This leads to expertise.

Who doesn't want to be an expert in something? Especially if it's an area you're already interested in naturally. As you develop your skills, more and more people will seek you out to advise them on your area of expertise, which could lead to countless new opportunities.

Your skill could be anything. From something as conventional as coding or website design to something unconventional like weaving or pottery. There will always be people who would want services across a wide range of industries and sectors. As long as you're at the top of yours, you'll always find opportunities to turn your passion into a business and make money from it.

## HOW CAN PASSION GENERATE NEW OPPORTUNITIES FOR YOU?

Adam Smith, one of the world's most famous economists, had put forth a simple proposition way back in the eighteenth century that's still valid today. He had said that as human civilization progresses, everyone will need specialized services that no one man can manage on his or her own. The answer to that would be everyone working for personal benefit, which will, in turn, lead to mutual benefit for the entire society.

The most classical example is that of the bread maker. Assume for a moment that you're a baker. Now, since you need clothes, other food items, a house etc., you start making bread, give it to other people, and get products and services in return from them. You get a mason to build you a house, in return for a lifetime supply of bread, and so on. Slowly and steadily, the modern monetary system developed to ease the transactions till we got to the modern system where everyone does one job and expects money in return for it and then uses that money to get other services.

So, by this proposition, one thing is clear. People need other people for goods and services. Assuming that you're good at what you do, which is easy to be if you're passionate about something and invest enough time and effort at it, people will always come to you with their requirements.

This is how things that you're passionate about can generate new opportunities for you and help you to chart your own course in life and career.

## HOW CAN YOU BECOME AN ENERGY POWER-HOUSE?

The easiest way to be an energy powerhouse is to have that energy come from within, from your drive and passion that fuels your desire to work.

Think about all the people you know who hate their job. They suffer from Monday Morning Blues, hate going to work and the highlight of their week is Friday when they get two days off of their job. Do you think that such people can ever be good employees or give 100% to their job? Of course not!

This comes from a distinct lack of passion toward what they do. Think about the one thing you love doing. It could be anything, maybe watching TV or playing a video game. Now think about the way you feel while you're waiting for the new episode, or going home to plug in your controller. Now, imagine if you could feel that way every morning before going to your office. That's what being passionate about your job does to you.

When you feel passionate about your job, nothing feels like a burden anymore. You're always looking forward to everything, even challenges. Assignments and presentation stop being chores and instead turn into what you love doing anyway, talking about what you feel passionate about.

Turning into an energy powerhouse is both easy and difficult. It's difficult because it requires you to figure out the one thing you're passionate about and then committing yourself to it. It's easy because once you have your passion in front of you, you'll never feel like your job is a burden or that you NEED to get something done, instead of desiring to work. Once you can get to that point in your life, no one can stop you from becoming an energy powerhouse.

## HOW CAN YOU FIND YOUR VISION THROUGH YOUR PASSION?

If an entrepreneur wants to see their vision and goals being accomplished, then their passion is the fuel that drives the production and results of the vision. The vision of the organization or team should be frequently and passionately communicated to others. Each member of the team should embrace that vision and have such pride in their work that they expect nothing but their best.

In this context, *a German once visited a temple under construction where he saw a sculptor making an idol of God. Suddenly, he noticed a similar idol lying nearby.*

*Surprised, he asked the sculptor, "Do you need two statues of the same idol?"*

*"No," said the sculptor without looking up, "We need only one, but the first one got damaged at the last stage."*

*The gentleman examined the idol and found no apparent damage.*

*"Where is the damage?" he asked.*

*"There's a scratch on the nose of the idol," said the sculptor, still busy with his work.*

*"Where are you going to install the idol?"*

*The sculptor replied that it would be installed on a pillar twenty feet high.*

*"If the idol is that high, who's going to know that there's a scratch on the nose?" the gentleman asked.*

*The sculptor stopped work, looked up at the gentleman, smiled, and said, "I will know it."*

*The desire to excel is exclusive of whether or not someone else appreciates it.*

*Similarly, passion is a drive from inside, not outside. Passion isn't for someone else to notice but for your own satisfaction and efficiency. Don't climb a mountain with an intention that the world should see you, climb the mountain with the intention to see the world.*

## HOW DOES PASSION INFLUENCE THE PEOPLE AROUND YOU?

When you become success, you become a leader, whether you want to be or not. That's because others will follow you, emulate you, and listen to your words, especially if you have a passion that inspires other. We've all seen or been around a passionate leader. I personally know that after I'm around a passionate leader, their energy and passions rub off on me. This causes me to feel more energized and motivated. A leader's passions can ignite other people's passion and bring energy into their life.

John Wesley said, "When you set yourself on fire, people love to come and see you burn." This is what happens when a leader has passion. The leader starts gaining more influence with others and people want to be a part of what's going on. If you want to raise your influence, then you need to be a passionate leader.

I've observed that an entrepreneur's passion brings new opportunity and opens the door to success. This is because being passionate about what you're doing moves you closer to your potential, and that causes you to be moving to the next level within your career and personal journey.

When you talk about your vision for the company, let your passion for your vision shine through. Others will feel it and want to get on board with you. If you don't have the passion for your vision, you need to recreate your vision or reframe the description of your vision so it's connected to your passion. We will have a more detailed discussion of vision and how it relates to passion in the chapter on Vision.

If you've been thinking, *I'm already following my passion*, while reading this chapter, that's great!

You should appreciate that because you're in the minority. According to The Conference Board, over 50% of Americans were dissatisfied with their jobs in 2010. It stated that most Americans were only working for their current employer simply because they had to. Now, obviously, most of us have to work one way or another (unless you were born into riches and are completely spoiled). So, don't just quit your day job because you aren't completely satisfied.

However, that doesn't mean you can't pursue another, more fulfilling, career path part time. Have you ever heard the saying, "It's never too late to be what you could've been?" Well, it's true. If you have an idea of where you desire to be, you can still make moves toward getting there. If you have a full-time job to support you while you make that transition, that may actually be even better. True success is much more than having a lot of wealth and fame. Enjoying the work you do is, in some ways, more important than having a large bank account.

Plus, if you enjoy the work you do, there's a greater chance you'll do great work and get paid accordingly.

If you're thinking about starting your own business or just struggling with this in your own personal career, you may need to think about what you're passionate about. It may not be easy, but chances are that it will be worth the effort.

*Once I got to college, I threw myself headfirst into my classes and assignments. I aced my first semester and was a favorite among my professors. However, all of that came at a cost. I was forcing myself to pay attention, to stay ahead of the class, spending hours in front of a book when the others understood the same thing in minutes. These were all warning signs, but I ignored them resolutely because of the weight of the responsibilities on me.*

*I barely got any sleep and didn't have a social life. I had lost touch with all of my friends from high school and I hadn't made any in college. I was on the cusp of burning out right at the end of my first semester.*

*My parents, worried about the frantic pace at which I was working, asked me to slow down a bit and find a hobby, something to take my mind off the stress of my classes. Too guilty and scared to do anything else, I turned to the library with a vengeance. If I was going to spend time away from my studies, I wasn't going to waste it over something meaningless. I had always liked reading, being the shy kid I was, and decided that it was the best hobby for me to save myself from burning out six months into college.*

*Even then, determined not to waste my time over "meaningless" novels, I turned to biographies and books on business and entrepreneurship. Call it a relapse if you will, but I gravitated toward them on my own. There were a thousand other books I could have chosen, but from the remaining bits and pieces of entrepreneurship in me, I started reading books on business extensively.*

*During the next semester, I experienced a stark shift in me as I slowly and steadily rediscovered my passion. I read every book on business I could lay my hands on from my college library. When the library ran out of titles I could read, I began borrowing from friends and buying old and used books from around the city. I started taking notes and looking for places to apply everything I had learned.*

*During this time, something else happened that pushed me further down this road. I invested all of my savings into a small business venture that I managed. It was simple enough. I would sell my class notes to others in my class. My grades in the previous semester supported my credentials, and people bought the notes from me. I made a good profit doing that. Soon enough, my entire class was studying from my notes for the exams. It was the first success I had tasted and it told me that I was good at business. I knew and understood people's needs and demands and had a way with words and with people. I could persuade them, cajole them, convince them, and, most importantly, sell to them. This was a soft turning point for me. I was suddenly reminded how it felt to be excited about what I love to do. I'd been studying engineering but had never felt excited about it the way working on this small business made me feel.*

*I fought this feeling. I hadn't forgotten what was at stake here. I was under debt; so was my father. My family had put a lot on the line, trying to send me here. I returned to my studies, determined to finish what I had started, constantly ignoring the small voice in the back of my head that was warning me that this wasn't what my true passion was.*

*I clearly remember the day when I finally went over the edge. It was during my third semester exams. The paper was on physics. However, instead of answering the questions and solving problems, I found myself doodling business ideas in the margin, looking for ways to make exams a more bearable process for people. As I caught myself doing that, I had an epiphany. This wasn't my calling. I had trudged along in engineering so far out of sheer stubbornness, but it was now time to come to terms with the fact that this wasn't what I was good at. If I stayed on this path, not only would I make myself miserable, I'd hurt my parents in the long run. My parents had sent me here to pursue my passion, but this wasn't what my passion had been all along; my passion had been something entirely different. I had been wrong, and it was now time to fix it.*

*I dropped out of college after the third semester. I took some time to clear my head and started working on a business idea. This is where the true story began. Finding the P in the P.O.W.E.R. to lead is easy. Following up on that is what scares most people away!*

# OPTIMISM

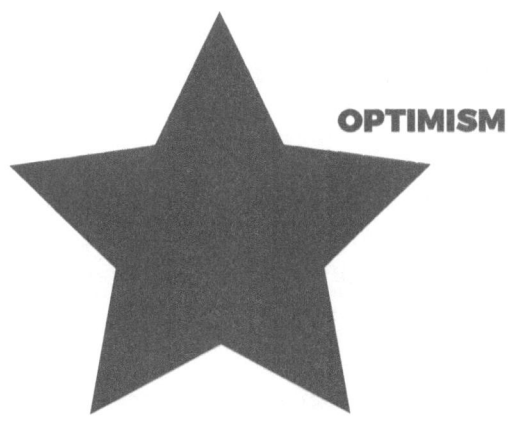

**OPTIMISM**

*Now, here was my situation. I had dropped out of college. I didn't have a lot of money saved up. I hadn't told my parents about my decision to drop out due to shame and guilt. And I didn't have a business plan to work on. All I knew was that I desired to start my own business and not waste any more of my money or time on college, knowing, for a fact, that it wasn't going to help in any way whatsoever in fulfilling my future plans.*

*Here, the most difficult part of my journey began. I'll get to it in the next chapter but there was a time when my business had failed. I was a twenty-year-old college dropout without a college degree and in debt. But even that wasn't as difficult as this next part of my journey.*

*When you're young, people always support your dreams. As you grow older, your dreams begin to terrify them. People find ways to pull you down if you drop out of the rat race and try to rise above others. They'll find creative ways to remind you that many have failed and make you believe that you'll fail too. This happened to me and will happen to you as well. If you're trying to start a business, taking any form of risk, or are doing anything that people in your community and society aren't doing, you'll hear naysayers trying to convince you to drop your idea.*

*I was no different. In my case, I got it even worse. I didn't have a plan. I didn't have the money to follow up on any plan either. My friends all made fun of me. I had to endure names like "Crazy" and "Insane" and these were the more polite ones.*

*It would have been really easy for me to go back. Return to college, pretend that whole episode never happened. No one would have found out a thing. In some weak moments, I was tempted to do so. All the ridicule gets to you eventually. We all take a long time to believe compliments but the insults and criticism, we're all too eager to believe. Soon enough, within a month or so, I found myself wondering if I should go back to college and drop this whole idea entirely.*

"You see things, and you say why? But I dream of things that never were, and I say why not?"—George Bernard Shaw.

"There are only two ways to live your life. One is as though nothing is a miracle. The other is as though everything is a miracle."—Albert Einstein

J. K. Rowling had twelve rejections of Harry Potter before someone accepted it and published it. Now she's the first billionaire author. We've learned from many people like her on many such countless occasions about optimism.

It's completely up to you that whether or not you make lemonade when life throws lemons at you. Whether you see a glass half empty, half full, or don't care and just drink the water, you have to stay positive whatever may be the cost. There are setbacks in our lives. Some are so small bumps that we don't even pay attention to, but others prove to be major roadblocks. Nevertheless, optimism is the key that can make you go the extra mile for good.

An optimist is someone who lives by the rule that there's nothing anyone else can do that they can't, and finally finds the light at the end of the tunnel.

Hundreds of studies have reported that optimists are happier, in better physical shape, have better sex, and live longer than pessimists. More importantly, from our point of view, they retain staff better and get better results than pessimists. Therefore, optimism is an important characteristic of successful visionary entrepreneurs.

But what exactly is optimism, and can you develop it, or are you born being optimistic?

Optimism is generally taken to mean an expectation that things will turn out well, that happy events will last and rub off on our lives as a whole, and that unfortunate events can be overcome. Pessimists feel the opposite, that the world is an unfriendly place and good events are aberrations.

These expectations may be based on experience, but the experiences are filtered through the explanations given to us by our parents, teachers, and friends – and our work culture.

Most studies report that the general phenomena of well-being, happiness, optimism, etc. are a fairly even mixture of genetic predisposition and learned behaviour, and that if you can learn it, you can learn it at any age.

However, optimism is a critical factor in effective entrepreneurship. Optimistic entrepreneurship isn't about being a Pollyanna. It isn't about denying reality. Rather, it's about the ability to remain committed to a vision in the face of adversity; it's about believing that the team can overcome adversity and still succeed.

entrepreneurs must be optimistic because the execution of a plan never happens without setbacks. When those setbacks occur, the optimistic powers break through.

Optimism can be seen as an emotional competence because it helps boost productivity, enhances employee morale, and overcomes challenges. Intel co-founder Robert Noyce once said that optimism is "an essential ingredient of innovation. How else can the individual welcome change over security, adventure over staying in safe places?"

Carmine Gallo, in an article in an August 8, 2012 article in Forbes, wrote, "Noyce and his partners started Intel in 1968, a year when the U.S economy faced the greatest crisis since the Great Depression. In addition, tumultuous events shook the foundation of American society: riots and protests, the Vietnam War, the assassinations of Martin Luther King and Robert Kennedy. It was a tough year to start a business, but Noyce embraced change and built a brand that changed the world."

As a business owner or administrator, the proverbial question: "Is the glass half empty or half full?" may not seem relevant to your concerns about managerial decision-making, employee retention, increased sales, and accountability, but the facts prove otherwise.

Optimism, as it turns out, makes a difference in these business measures as well as productivity, customer satisfaction, and profit. Why is this? Essentially, when pessimistic people run into the inevitable obstacle, they give up. After all, they never expected it to succeed in the first place. Conversely, when optimistic people encounter obstacles, they try harder.

Instead of giving up, they find ways to handle the obstacle and reach their objective. In addition, because optimists expect things to turn out well, they generate more positive outcomes. In today's workplace, business acumen and professional skills aren't enough to guarantee success. If you want to outperform the competition and reach optimal potential, then cultivating optimism is the answer.

But you might say, "Aren't those employees who always see the glass as half full just deluding themselves?" To answer this question, let's get clear about what I mean by optimism. Fostering an optimistic work environment doesn't mean that everyone turns into a "Pollyanna" and operates on blind faith that everything will "turn out fine." Neither does it mean that employees operate on wishful thinking, striving for unattainable goals, and focusing on fantasy desires. I'm not talking about optimists who are dogmatic, ignoring any discouraging signs and only focusing on positive aspects. Neither am I talking about optimists who are irrational, throwing caution to the wind, and overlooking the need for risk assessment.

Having a positive attitude won't help you accomplish anything, it won't make you a million dollars, it won't turn you into an astronaut, and it won't let you fly a plane around the world. However, it will certainly help you do everything better than a negative attitude will.

The optimists who are needed in today's workplace embody qualities that include self-awareness, flexibility, self-confidence, initiative, resilience, and adaptability. Whether CEO, manager, or line staff, these optimists employ a system of thinking, feeling, and behaving that creates conditions for success. Their optimistic attitude allows them to recognize and redirect unproductive reactions, think before acting and choose beneficial responses. Their optimism equips them with a perspective that fosters personal accountability, innovative thinking, and appropriate risk-taking.

## HOW CAN YOU TURN A BUSINESS PROBLEM INTO AN OPPORTUNITY?

An optimist sees opportunity where others see uncertainty and despair. When the economy was down a few year ago and millions of people were out of work, the pessimist used those factors as excuses to stay in place. The optimist refuses to let macroeconomic trends impose hurdles on their imagination. Nothing will dissuade them from starting businesses that ultimately put people to work. As Winston Churchill once said, "Optimists see opportunities in every difficulty." Optimists have a successful mind-set. You simply cannot start a successful business in a difficult economic environment unless you cast off the negative emotions of fear, uncertainty, and worry.

On top of that, every business problem is an opportunity. Think about it. If you could get the job done easily, so could your competitors. Then, what incentive would any business or customer have to come to you with their requirements? They could get it done by anyone who did it for the cheapest rate.

The very fact that you're struggling with a challenge means that the skill isn't very common and your customer has access to a much smaller pool of businesses that can get the job done. This means that you not only can get more money to do the job but also that the customer will always come back to you for any further needs.

Still thinking that business problems aren't opportunities?

## HOW CAN YOU PERSUADE PEOPLE FOR GOOD?

The word inspiration means, "To elicit a fervent enthusiasm." You cannot elicit enthusiasm for an idea unless you're a strong communicator. It's no coincidence that Ronald Reagan, one of the most optimistic Americans we'll ever know, was called "the great communicator." Colin Powell served under Reagan and said that optimism was the secret behind Reagan's charisma.

In fact, everyone who knew Reagan described him as an eternal optimist, someone who believed in a better future. I work directly with some of the world's best communicators. Every one of them is more optimistic than the average person.

Reagan had his share of skeptics but his speeches brought out the best in people. They wanted to live in the world he painted with his words. Another optimist, Winston Churchill, also faced skeptics. In Churchill's case, nearly the entire British population was skeptical about going to war with Nazi Germany. Churchill single-handedly turned around public opinion in World War II with a series of optimistic speeches, painting a picture of how Britain could turn back the Nazi tide washing over Europe.

In a matter of weeks, the British attitude shifted from one of appeasement to one of certainty that they could fight and win. Members of Churchill's wartime cabinet said his words and attitude made people feel braver in his presence.

## HOW CAN YOU DEVELOP A NEVER QUIT, NO MATTER WHAT ATTITUDE?

When Jim Carrey was fourteen years old, his father lost his job, and his family hit rough times. They moved into a VW van on a relative's lawn and the young aspiring comedian, who was so dedicated to his craft that he mailed his resume to The Carol Burnett Show just a few years earlier, at age ten, took an eight-hours-per-day factory job after school to help make ends meet.

At age fifteen, Carrey performed his comedy routine onstage for the first time in a suit his mom made for him and totally bombed, but he was undeterred. The following year, at sixteen, he quit school to focus on comedy full time. Shortly after, he moved to LA where he would park on Mulholland Drive every night and visualize his success. One of those nights, he wrote himself a check for $10,000,000 for "Acting Services Rendered," which he dated for Thanksgiving, 1995. Just before that date, he hit his payday with Dumb and

Dumber. He put the deteriorated check, which he'd kept in his wallet the whole time, in his father's casket.

In another aspect, we all need optimists in our lives to fight the "recency effect." The recency effect is a psychological term that simply means the most recent experiences we go through are the ones we're likely to remember and we assume those experiences will continue into the future.

It's the primary reason why investors pull their money out of stocks when the market goes down and put their money in when the market is nearing a high. As any astute investor will tell you, that's exactly the wrong way to invest in the market.

We need entrepreneurs who are immune to the "recency effect" and who see the big picture, reminding us of the long term. No recession is ever as bad as it seems at the moment. If you're surrounded by pessimists, you're likely to assume that nothing will get better, whether it's the economy, or your personal situation.

## HOW CAN YOU HELP PEOPLE EVOLVE?

In Colin Powell's new book, *It Worked for Me: In Life and Leadership,* he says that great leaders know things will get better because they themselves will make them better!

*A little boy went to a phone booth that was at the cash counter of a store, and dialed a number.*

*The store owner observed and listened to half of the conversation:*

*Boy: "Lady, can you give me the job of cutting your lawn?"*

*Woman (at the other end of the phone line): "I already have someone to cut my lawn."*

*Boy: "Lady, I'll cut your lawn for half the price than the person who cuts your lawn now."*

*Woman: "I'm very satisfied with the person who's presently cutting my lawn."*

*Boy: (with more perseverance) "Lady, I'll even sweep the floor and the stairs of your house for free."*

*Woman: "No, thank you."*

*With a smile on his face, the little boy ends the call, saying thank you."*

*The store owner walked over to the boy.*

*Store Owner: "Son...I like your attitude; I like that positive spirit and would like to offer you a job."*

*Boy: "No, thanks."*

*Store Owner: "But you were really pleading for one."*

*Boy: "No, Sir, I was just checking my performance at the job I already have. I'm the one who's working for that lady I was talking to!"*

*This is optimism.*

Powell says military training is the best preparation for approaching difficult situations with an optimistic outlook. The following was drilled into Powell: "Lieutenant, you may be starving but you must never show hunger. You may be freezing or near heat exhaustion but you must never show that you're cold or hot. You may be terrified but you must never show fear. You're the leader, and the troops will reflect your emotions." People must believe that no matter how bad things look, you'll make them better.

An added plus in the workplace is the fact that optimism makes you smarter. Researchers have shown that positive emotions actually fuel creativity and enhance your reasoning skills, creating more successful results. This is because a positive mood changes the way your brain processes information. If you're under stress, feel beaten down, or are in a sad mood, your brain hunkers down. You become more detached and cautious because your brain focuses on what's wrong and how to eliminate it. On the other hand, when you're in a relaxed, cheerful mood, your brain opens up. More neurons fire; thus, your brain is likely to enter into a creative, exploratory state. You begin to seek out new experiences in your environment. You feel expansive, generous, tolerant, and productive.

## HOW CAN YOU BE OPTIMISTIC AND BE UNIMAGINABLY HAPPY?

And here's even more good news. Optimism can be learned. Natural optimists can cultivate more optimism and born pessimists can become 50% more optimistic by learning how to choose thoughts, feelings, and behaviors that put them on an upward spiral. I'll illustrate this with a short story.

*There was a king who had one eye and one leg.*

*He asked all the painters to draw a beautiful portrait of him but none of them could. How could they paint him beautifully with the defects in one eye and one leg?*

*Eventually, one of them agreed and drew a classic picture of the king.*

*It was a fantastic picture that surprised everyone.*

*He painted the king aiming for a hunt. He was shown targeting with one eye closed and one leg bent.*

So, why can't we all paint pictures like this for others? Hiding their weakness and highlighting their strengths?

How can you or the people you manage become more optimistic? Employees can acquire the tools for creating success in the workplace by learning to ask five important questions that allow them to adapt to changes and respond to the new demands of today's competitive marketplace. These are:

1. *What can I do to achieve the best possible outcome?*

2. *What are the innovative responses to the situation?*

3. *What do I need to know to reach a productive conclusion?*

4. *What can I learn from this situation that will help me in the future?*

5. *What is an interpretation of this event that will motivate me to continue to strive for excellence and success?*

By employing strategies that allow you to put these questions into practice, you become more adept at handling any situation that might arise. When things don't go your way, don't waste time and energy thinking, *This always happens to me. I can never get a break.* This kind of thinking leads to inaction, helplessness, avoidance, and conflict in the workplace. Instead, respond to a difficult situation by focusing your energy on areas of the situation that can be controlled. *Figure out ways to solve problems creatively and appraise events objectively in order to find beneficial actions.* When there's a setback or mistake, look for insights that will help you improve. Approach difficulties by looking for potential gains.

Managers who are optimistic raise the aspirations of people to achieve their individual best by focusing on innovation, problem solving, and creative failures. Customer-service representatives who are optimistic are more likely to connect with the customer and ensure a positive outcome to interactions. Line staffs who are optimistic will be able to find the positive when the inevitable changes occur in policies and procedures. Salespeople who are optimistic will make more sales.

Charles Schultz said, "Life is like a ten-speed bike. Most of us have gears we never use."

By exemplifying, teaching, and fostering optimism in the workplace, you help your employees tap into and use their full potential as you unleash your own capacity for success.

In *The Rational Optimist*, Matt Ridley describes how, if we look at the world rationally, there's no other conclusion than the fact that we're living in an unprecedented era of prosperity. Yes, there are some places that are worse off. "The vast majority are much better fed, much better sheltered, much better entertained, much better protected against disease and much more likely to live to old age than their ancestors have ever been." Your employees are looking *to you for inspiration and they're not getting it from the news headlines. The media tends to focus on bad news because bad news sells. But you know what? Good news also sells and makes people feel better.*

So, as long as you're alive, try to look at the world optimistically. Never let anyone stop you from being optimistic. Never tell yourself that you can't do it. If it's not one thing, it's another.

As we move on to the next chapter, here's an optimistic fact for you,

"The percentage of women in parliament has nearly doubled in the last twenty years," according to the annual report of the Inter-Parliamentary Union (IPU) a UN partner agency.

*Luck has a strange enough way of working. If I had to live like that, without a plan, and with all this ridicule from my closest friends for a few more months, I would have quit on my dreams and returned to doing what was expected of me. Destiny, however, had other plans in mind.*

*One evening, I received a call from my father. He had retired from his job in the military and was now looking for something else to do with his free time. We got talking and, soon enough, he mentioned that he was looking to get into the real estate business. I was elated! I encouraged him to do it and that I'd get him all the contacts he needed. He mentioned that there was a small problem of capital. Due to the fact that we came from a humble, middle class background, we didn't have enough money to invest in something as capital intensive as real estate. He said that he had been looking for investors but hadn't been able to find any.*

*This was my eureka moment. After I had hung up and was lying awake in the middle of the night, I realized that there must be a lot of other entrepreneurs who didn't have the contacts to meet investors, and, at the same time, there must be a lot of investors who, due to lack of time or contacts couldn't find a suitable business to invest in. My idea was to create a forum to bring investors and entrepreneurs together.*

*Now that I had my idea, I hit the next snag in the plan. I knew nothing about how to get all of this done. I didn't know anything about website design, creating and running a company, SEO, or Internet advertising. All I had was an idea, not even an original one when I look back upon it now, and that was it.*

*Sometimes, I look back and wonder how life would have been different if I hadn't received that call that day. It was an unusual conversation too. My father had never really talked about his career or money with me. It was highly unusual for us to have had that conversation that day, but, somehow, we did, and that set me upon the path that I'm still walking on today.*

*Optimism is the most difficult part of P.O.W.E.R.. The others, like Passion, come to you and once you've acquired them, they stay with you. Not optimism. To stay optimistic is a constant uphill battle and one that never ends, even when you have an established profitable business. Negativity can set in anytime and you become pessimistic; then it's very difficult to make yourself see things positively again.*

*There's also the danger of false or misplaced optimism. You could be optimistic that someday things will fly upwards. That's a fool's hope. In this case, we have laws of gravity to let us know that we'll be wrong, but in the other cases, like that of a business idea, you can never really know when you have a pipe dream that's never going to succeed.*

*The answer is optimism and faith. Have faith in yourself and your idea and start working. Something good would come out of it anyway. As Oscar Wilde said, "Experience is simply the name we give our mistakes."*

# WILLPOWER

**WILLPOWER**

*Now, I had a plan, and nothing else. I didn't have the technical knowledge to set up the website; neither did I have the savings to hire a team to do it for me. However, all the reading that I'd done in college came back to my aid. I knew, from back then, that given enough time, you could learn absolutely anything from books. I threw myself in.*

*I bought books on Web design, domain hosting, html programming, everything that I needed to know in order to create the forum I'd been planning to do. I hired a few people to help me with the content writing part of things, while, at the same time, I threw in my savings to get my company registered (a bad move in retrospect, but more on that later).*

*Once I had the website up and running, I didn't know a whole lot about marketing and advertising it. I also didn't realize how stiff the competition was out there in this industry. Many different websites worked on the same project and had directories of thousands of investors and businesses. In contrast, mine was a new website with a directory of less than a hundred or so people. Thus, it wasn't very lucrative to either investors or businesses.*

*Once again, I threw myself into it. I read everything I could on advertising and marketing. I promoted my website like a madman. I showed up at every convention and seminar in town where businesses or investors were supposed to show up and gave them my card. Some of them called me back; some registered for the website. My company was growing; but I hit a problem I hadn't foreseen, mostly due to lack of experience and naive idealism.*

*Any website of this sort, unless it's working on a niche with no competition whatsoever and has a first mover advantage, needs some time to gain traction amongst the users. The Internet, though it's a global marketplace, has its own problems of discoverability. It takes a while before any website is discovered by enough people to gain traction and start to attract traffic organically. Of course, I didn't known this back then. I had been under the impression that once I set up the website, I'd be able to break even in a quarter. That wasn't likely anymore from what I was seeing.*

*Gong Fu is an ancient Chinese term describing work, devotion, and effort, which, in turn, points to Willpower that has been successfully applied over a substantial length of time, resulting in a degree of mastery in a specific field. The term is associated in the West with martial arts; it's most often spelled Kung Fu.*

# HOW CAN YOU ATTAIN SELF-DISCIPLINE & ACHIEVE WHATEVER YOU DESIRE IN YOUR LIFE?

Willpower is the ability to control unnecessary and harmful impulses. It's the ability to overcome laziness and procrastination.

It's the ability to arrive at a decision and follow through with perseverance until you reach a successful accomplishment. It's the inner power that overcomes the desire to indulge in unnecessary and useless habits and the inner strength that overcomes inner emotional and mental resistance to taking action. It's one of the cornerstones of success, both spiritual and material.

Self-discipline is the companion of willpower. It bestows the stamina to persevere in whatever one does. It confers the ability to withstand hardships and difficulties, whether physical, emotional, or mental. It grants one the ability to reject immediate satisfaction for something better.

A human being is full of unconscious or partly conscious impulses. People sometimes say or do things they later regret saying or doing. On many occasions, people don't think before they talk or act.

By developing these two powers, people become conscious of their inner subconscious impulses and gain the ability to reject them when they're not for their own good.

Willpower and self-discipline helps us to choose our behavior and reactions instead of being their slaves. Don't think that life will become dull and dry in this way. On the contrary, you'll feel more powerful, in charge of yourself and your surroundings, and, consequently, much more happy and satisfied.

How many times have you felt too weak, lazy, or shy to do something you needed to do? You can gain inner strength and the ability to decide whether to act or react, or refuse to act or react in any situation. Believe me; it's not difficult to develop these two powers. If you're earnest and are willing to become stronger, you'll certainly succeed.

The importance of willpower is recognized by most people, yet, few deliberately give any time or thought to its development. Why we resist one thing and yield to another may be due to which one has the stronger appeal, but what more particularly concerns us in the study of self-confidence is a way this mighty power can be built and directed.

In this section, you'll find some exercises and techniques to develop these abilities. You can perform these exercises anywhere and at any time. Go slowly and gradually and your powers will increase. The desire and ambition to practice these exercise will develop and strengthen your self-discipline.

One way to develop and improve this ability is to practice doing disagreeable things in your daily life. Your mind and feelings may oppose this action but, nevertheless, do it. By doing something you don't like or are too lazy to do, you overcome your subconscious resistances, train your inner powers, and gain strength. Muscles get stronger by resisting the power of the barbells. Inner strength is attained by overcoming inner resistance.

## ACTIONABLE EXERCISES FOR YOU TO DEVELOP WILLPOWER IN AN EASY WAY:

1) *You're sitting on a bus or train and an old man or woman, or a pregnant lady walks in. Stand up and give up your seat, even if you prefer to stay seated. Do this not just because it's polite but because you're doing something that you're reluctant to do. In this way, you're overcoming the resistance of your body, mind, and feelings.*

2) *There are dishes on the sink that needs washing and you postpone washing them for later. Get up and wash them now. Don't let your laziness overcome you. When you know this is a successful way to develop your willpower, and if you're convinced of the importance of willpower in your life, it will be easier for you to do whatever you have to do.*

3) *You come home tired from work and sit in front of the TV because you feel too lazy and tired to take a shower. Don't obey the inclination to just sit but take a shower.*

4) *You may know your body needs some physical exercise, but,*

*instead, you keep on sitting, doing nothing or watching a movie. Get up & walk, run, or do some other physical exercise.*

5) *Do you like your coffee with sugar? Then, for a whole week, decide to drink it without sugar. Do you like to drink three cups of coffee each day? For a week, drink only two.*

6) *Overcome your laziness and your habits. Convince yourself of the importance of what needs to be done. Convince your mind that you become stronger when you do chores, even when you're reluctant, too lazy, or feel that you're too tired.*

7) *Sometimes, when you want to say something that's not important, decide not to say it.*

8) *Don't read some unimportant gossip in the newspaper, even if you want to.*

9) *You have a craving to eat something not too healthy. Refuse the craving.*

10) *If you find yourself thinking unimportant, unnecessary, negative thoughts, try to develop a lack of interest in them by persuading yourself of their futility.*

# HOW TO BE THE BOSS OF YOUR OWN MIND!

Never say that you cannot follow the above exercises because you certainly can. Be persistent, no matter what. Think and rethink about the importance of performing the exercises and the inner power and strength they'll give you. Believe me, it helps. It helped me and it can help you.

Trying to attempt too many exercises immediately at the start may end in disappointment. It's better to start with small and not so important actions at first and gradually increase the number and difficulty of the exercises. Practice will improve and increase your power, giving you a lot of satisfaction.

Remember, these exercises develop both willpower and self-discipline as they're intimately connected. Strengthening one strengthens the other.

Most of these exercises can be practiced anywhere, anytime. You don't have to devote special time for them. Trust my experience; they're very effective. Practicing them enables you to be strong and exercise willpower and self-discipline in everything you do. This power becomes available whenever needed.

If you practice weight lifting, running, or aerobics, you strengthen your body. When you need to move something heavy, you have the strength for it. By studying French each day, you'll be able to speak French when you travel to France. The same thing happens with willpower and self-discipline. By strengthening them, they become available whenever they're needed.

The exercises should be practiced because of your decision to perform them, and because you realize that by doing them you'll develop your willpower and self-discipline.

One important thing to remember is to not interfere with your health or deny your body and its necessities. Deny what isn't necessary or harmful and you'll get stronger.

If you stop doing something in order to strengthen yourself and you find that it's easy, you can resume doing it if it isn't harmful. For example, you love taking a hot shower, and in order to strengthen your willpower, you switch to cold showers. You then find out that after the first few seconds, you get used to it and it wakes you up and invigorates you. You can keep taking cold showers or switch back to hot showers if you like. You've proven to yourself that you're stronger than your subconscious impulses. Always use your reason and common sense so that you do no damage to yourself. For example, if you have a heart condition, don't take cold showers.

Willpower gets stronger by holding back and not allowing the expression of unimportant, unnecessary and unhealthy thoughts, feelings, actions, and reactions. If this saved energy isn't allowed expression, it's stored inside you like a battery and it becomes available at the time of need. By practicing the exercises, you develop your powers the same way as someone who engages in bodybuilding builds his muscles. When you exercise your willpower, you strengthen your self-discipline and gain inner strength. The more you exercise, the stronger you become.

You need both willpower and self-discipline to rule your thoughts, and this is how you turn out to be the "boss of your mind."

The stronger your thoughts, the more control you have over them and, consequently, your powers of concentration get stronger.

When you're the master of your mind, you enjoy inner peace and happiness. Outer events don't sway you and circumstances have no power over your peace of mind. It may sound like a dream for you, but once you start on the way, you'll prove to yourself that all the above is true.

They're essential for self-growth, spiritual growth and meditation. They're the powers that change your habits and are the keys to any kind of success.

Willpower and self-discipline give you more control over your daily life and help you in the development of all the inner powers that are essential for a spiritual search. They keep you on the right track until you get what you're after.

There are many things we desire to avoid, such as poverty, pain, misfortune, and ill-health; and there are things we much desire to have, such as wealth, power, knowledge, and independence. However, the intensity of our desire is what counts for most.

## HOW TO BE WHAT YOU DESIRE TO BE.

"I desire to become a good public speaker," says the student.

"How strong is your desire?" asks the teacher. "Will you practice regularly every day for an hour?"

"I don't think I can," says, the student "because I'm too busy during the day, and, at night, I'm too tired."

"What personal sacrifices are you ready to make?"

"None," is the answer.

"Then", replies the teacher, "Your desire isn't strong enough to make you a good public speaker."

This applies with equal force to you, dear reader, in terms of developing your self-confidence. Does desire control the will or does will control desire? Psychologists point to consciousness as confirming our freedom to choose a certain course and pursue it, with the feeling that we could choose some other course if we so desired.

In either event, there's no feeling of compulsion, and this would seem to confirm the idea of free will.

Let desire, then, be the starting point of the attempt to educate your will. To strengthen immediately your desire for a strong will, you should dwell intently upon the advantages this power will confer. You should think deeply upon the satisfaction that will come from doing things definitely and promptly and the increased self-confidence that will surely follow from the habit of finishing in a thorough manner in everything that you undertake.

By dwelling long and earnestly upon the inestimable value of a strong, well-directed will, you will develop an intense desire to possess this faculty, use it daily, and finally, by its aid, realize your life's ambition.

Don't put yourself in temptation's way, or, if you can't avoid it, make it harder for yourself to succumb. Use your willpower actively: plan, commit, and do so (like members of religious communities) publicly. "People with low willpower," Baumeister says, "use it to get themselves out of crises. People with high willpower use it not to get themselves into crises."

The will to succeed leads you to success. Forget about your struggle, where you come from or what you look like; your determination to do something is what makes you successful.

*"In a recent survey of 1,200 professionals, 88% said receiving praise from a manager was either 'very' or 'extremely' rewarding and recognition was more fulfilling than financial*

*rewards,"* according to Victor Lipman in a June 13, 2013 Psychology Today article.

*This was where my troubles started. I didn't have enough money to keep my employees on the payroll, my savings were used up, and I was in debt. On top of that, the money wasn't going to come in for another year or so, maybe even more. Keeping the website up and running would have been difficult for me without any revenue coming in. I had to make a hard decision here. I could keep the website running and run myself deeper in debt by paying salaries of three people, advertisement space, and other overheads. Or I could shut down and cut my losses then and there.*

*Many people misunderstand willpower. They think of it as pushing on even when the odds are stacked against them no matter what comes. This is true, but it's also true that you need to pick your fights carefully. Willing yourself to fight a fight that you know you'll lose is no demonstration of willpower. That's a demonstration of stupidity. I was strong willed but, at the same time, I decided that I wouldn't be stupid.*

*I closed down the company. At the end of the first year, this was my condition. My first business venture had failed spectacularly. I had run through all of my savings and, at the same time, managed to chalk up a significant amount of debt. On top of that, I was back to square one, right where I started from. I still had no college degree, no ideas, and no significantly increased technical expertise. On top of that, I had been lying to my parents.*

*That was, arguably, the lowest point of my journey. But, as they say, once you've hit rock bottom, you can only go up. That's exactly what I did, and that's what you'll see in the next chapter why the E in the P.O.W.E.R. is the most important element of them all. The others are important too, of course, and you cannot really do away with them but it's the E in P.O.W.E.R. that ensures that you keep on going, even more so than Willpower. Willpower is what gets you started on your journey. Whether you stay on your chosen path or not, is a different story with different characters.*

# ENDURANCE

**ENDURANCE**

*As soon as I shut down the company and wrapped it all up, I decided to go home for a while to get my mind off of things and get back in the game with a fresh start. On top of that, I still hadn't told my parents that I had dropped out of college, so the guilt was killing me as well. I decided that, come what may, I would tell my parents everything that had happened and come clean.*

*The day I told my parents about quitting college, starting a business, failing at it, and being in debt was, by far, the worst day of my life.*

*My father had been in the army. He was a man's man. I had never seen him bend, become upset, or lose his cool. Whatever might be happening around him, the entire world could be on fire and he wouldn't lose his cool and focus on getting the job done. The day when I told him everything, he listened to everything without saying a word. When I was done speaking, he silently got up, went into his study, and locked the door. He didn't come out for an entire day.*

*Even when I came back, my struggle was far from over. I had seen heartbreak from my family, now it was time to face ridicule. I had been sharing a dorm with a few friends who were still in college and they were convinced that I was insane. In retrospect, I can't blame them. I used to stay locked in my room, sometimes for days at a time, planning for my next venture, thinking of ideas, marketing strategies, products, and vertical I could get in.*

*Professionally as well, I wasn't getting anywhere. I was getting rejected by investors left and right. I remembered one investor actually yelled me to get out of his office five minutes into the meeting. My first product had been a dud and I wasn't sure what I wanted to work on next. On top of that, I was also in debt. But all of that had been nothing to the real thorn in my side.*

*You haven't known pain until you see people you love the most cry because of your bad choices. That day, I realized that everything I had gone through till then, the dropping out, the debt, the failure, couldn't compare to the way my heart was torn out of my chest on seeing my father cry. At this hardest point in my journey, I decided that, whatever happened, this would be the last time I'd hurt my family. I had to succeed now. There was no other option for me.*

Endurance is definitely the hardest element to acquire, and it's harder yet to keep going in the face of adversity. I know it might sound counterintuitive to you, considering I had advised you in the last chapter to cut your losses and not fight that which you cannot possibly win. Yet, at the same time, Enduring through the early blows of a fight where you have a chance is the most important difference between success and failure. No doubt, you will encounter difficulty when you start. You'll have to face failure, you'll have no money coming in, and you will be tempted to take the easy way out. But enduring through all of that is what will make you succeed in the long run.

Thomas Edison went through thousands of failures before he perfected the light bulb. He said, "I have not failed. I've just found 10,000 ways that won't work." If he hadn't endured past those initial failures to finally invent the electric light bulb, you might be reading this by candlelight.

J. K. Rowling, before she published the Harry Potter series of novels, was nearly penniless, severely depressed, divorced, and trying to raise a child on her own while attending school and writing a novel. She went from surviving on welfare to thriving as the first billionaire author and richest women in the world in a period of only five years through her hard work and determination.

Walt Disney had many personal failures. He was fired by a newspaper editor because, "he lacked imagination and had no good ideas." After that, Disney started a number of businesses that didn't last too long and ended with bankruptcy and failure. He had his Oswald the Rabbit stolen from him. But he kept trying and learning and soon create Mickey Mouse.

*If you look at the stories of successful entrepreneurs, you'll see that they've all failed. But only by enduring those failures and not letting those failures break them down or dishearten them were they able to build their empires. One way to look at it is that success is going from one failure to another without the loss of enthusiasm. And once you've managed to endure one failure, you'll be surprised at how unfazed you'll be in the face of your next adversity.*

## WHAT TRAIT SHOULD YOU DEVELOP FOR NEVER LOSING IN LIFE?

The answer is simple but not easy. Let me explain. What you need to do for never losing in life is really simple and obvious to understand. Implementing it, on the other hand, is really difficult and usually takes a lot out of you.

Also, never losing in life doesn't talk about the small setbacks. It's impossible to succeed at everything in life at the first go. If you do, you're not stepping out of your comfort zone and expanding your horizons. This way, you'll end up getting yourself stuck in a rut where you're good at a very few selected things and would have no idea how to deal with the other issues that might come up. In today's world where change is so rapid and quick, getting yourself stuck in a rut is an extremely dangerous thing to do. It might just so happen that in a few years, the skills you're good at might become obsolete due to some new advances in technology. Therefore, don't get stuck, and always keep on moving forward and learning new things.

*However, learning new things and taking risks inevitably means some failures and setbacks in the beginning. Endurance is what keeps you going through those and that's the one trait you need to never lose in life.*

*Losing can be easily defined as the difference between the number of times you fall down and the number of times you get up. As long as you keep the number of times you get up to get back in the game, just one more than the times you get knocked down, nothing can defeat you in the game of life. Losing happens when you quit trying. Life doesn't have a set of rules to define winning or losing. You draw your own rules, and, if you're playing on your own rules, you don't really have an option of quitting.*

*Endurance is the one trait that you need to develop in yourself to ensure that no matter what happens, you don't quit and keep on fighting against the odds stacked against you.*

## **WHAT ENDURANCE CAN DO FOR YOU?**

I guess we've all heard the story about a man who was digging in his backyard looking for gold during the California Gold Rush. He kept digging for a few days, and, when he didn't find anything in the first few feet, he gave up and sold his land to someone else. That man started digging too, even though the previous owner had told him that there was nothing in there. He continued digging and, a few weeks later, hit a literal gold mine. The rest is history.

What lessons can you take away from this story? One is the danger of quitting too soon. You could be feet or days away from a breakthrough and end up losing it simply because you quit too soon. Two is learning to trust your instincts.

More people quit because it's the logical thing to do rather than it's what their gut says. Many more push on, even when their gut has been telling them to quit. They rationalize their actions and continue throwing in resources after a sunk cost, trying to salvage it, when what they should be doing is cutting their losses.

Endurance is what separates winners from losers. Enduring a situation is usually difficult, but enduring a tough situation, riding out a big wave, can also be a wonderful opportunity for your business to grow.

Think of it this way. There are two reasons why your business could be in a tough spot. There could be a slump in the industry or your business could be losing out due to tough competition on internal inefficiencies. Enduring these tough situations could be good for you in every way when you think about it.

If your business is down due to a slump in the industry, it would be the perfect time to innovate. If you can recognize the factors leading to the slump and come up with a solution to fix that, you could essentially capture the entire market before your competition even begins to move.

On the other hand, if you're suffering due to tough competition, then revamping your strategies, product, and team could make your business more efficient, which would help you not only capture more market in time but also create more value for your customers, which will only lead to more business.

This applies to every facet of your life. Tough situations don't last, but tough people do. And the people who outlast those tough situations are the people who end up winning in the long run.

## WHICH FIGHTS ARE WORTH FIGHTING?

Enduring a losing battle is just as bad as not enduring a battle you can win.

There will be times when you'll be faced with situations that can't be won, irrespective of how much time or effort you throw at it. The reasons could be various. Maybe the correct technology doesn't exist yet, you don't have the right set of people working on the problem, or the timing isn't right. In such cases, instead of throwing time and money into a cause that has low chances of coming through, you would be better off investing those resources elsewhere.

But how would you know which fights are worth fighting? Well, that's where your instincts come in. Instinct is developed over the course of your career (another reason why experience is highly sought after in any job). Assuming you're an entrepreneur, you'll have to develop your instincts so that you can recognize a lost cause from a distance and act on it.

Another important aspect of this is to understand which

decisions are coming from your gut and which from rationalizing your actions. In many cases, instincts are very strong predictors of problems or opportunities (a very interesting read on the subject is Blink by Malcolm Gladwell if you want to explore this idea in more depth). You need to recognize how to separate the decisions coming from your gut from the ones you consciously think and deliberate upon. This can only come with experience, and, for that, you'll have to step onto the battlefield.

## HOW TO ENDURE AND STAY STRONG IN YOUR LIFE

We've established so far why Endurance is important, but not a lot has been said about how to endure a situation. It's well known that everything is easier said than done. So enduring a difficult situation, in itself, is an art and one that requires you to call upon all the other qualities we've talked about so far. It's obvious how willpower is important to your ability to endure.

But your greatest ally in enduring a tough situation is Optimism. Optimism can ease your journey greatly as you struggle with a situation or problem. Just by believing that you'll get over the problem can help a lot in keeping you positive and trying different things to solve the problem. However, this will only help you once you can differentiate between a good fight and a bad one. If you cannot, then staying optimistic will only make matters worse for you by getting you to dig deeper into the hole you cannot escape from.

A very good way to stay optimistic is by meditating. It can also help you find your passion. When I was going through the roughest patches of my journey, meditation really helped me connect with my inner self and discover who I truly was. Now, before you write it off as new-age mumbo jumbo, let me explain what I mean by that. Most people have abilities and aptitudes they are born with or learn, and they believe they have or can develop other abilities and aptitudes. These are two starkly different things for most people, and the sooner you realize the difference between the two, the happier and more productive you'll be. If you think you're a great web designer but your true talent is writing, you'll be better off working on writing content instead of designing websites. And this example can be extrapolated to all the spheres of your life. This is also where your passion comes into play.

# HOW TO STAND AGAINST ALL ODDS

Endurance is standing against all odds when you think about it. Irrelevant of the facet of life that you use endurance for, it's essentially the ability to stand tall in the face of adversity and continue doing your own thing, even when the odds are stacked against you.

What does the phrase, odds stacked against you, mean in the first place? It means that if you look at the individual factors that would lead to your success, they're all working against you. Maybe your competition has a bigger funding, your team isn't working to its fullest potential, or the deal you needed fell through. All these are enough to make anyone give up and look for other ways. But that's exactly what Endurance is: not giving up when everything is telling you to.

Consider the movie Rocky, the most classic underdog story about having the odds stacked up against you. At one point, Rocky says, "It's about how hard you can get hit and keep moving forward, how much you can take and keep moving forward. That's how winning is done!"

That's all there is to endurance. When the world is beating you down and you have no reason to continue fighting yet you still choose to fight, that's what enduring is, and that's something all winners in life have done. Steve Jobs could have quit after he was fired from Apple. Instead, he started Pixar and won back his fortune. Zuckerberg could have quitted when he was sued by his own friends for stealing their website. Instead, he endured all that and now is one of the richest people on the planet.

The easiest way to endure something is simple. Keep the beginning and end in your mind always. The ups and downs are a part of every story. That's what makes a good story. But as long as you have a clear idea of why you started and where you desired to go, enduring everything else would become much easier. Your end game, your vision, your dream that would keep you going. If you truly believe in your dream and truly care about your vision, no hardship can be difficult enough to make you quit. They would be inconveniences, annoyances, distractions, but never something that would force you to throw in the towel and give up on your dreams. We'll talk more about Vision and your Why in the last chapter.

So the way to endure hardships is simple, but it's not easy at all. It takes a lot of strength of character and conviction in your dreams to not quit on them when you face problems. Always remember that it's very easy to quit but the quitters aren't the people who are remembered. No songs are sung, no books are written, and no movies are made about the people who gave up midway on their fight. As a successful leader, your people need you to endure. You owe it to yourself and them to keep on keeping on. So, for you own dreams as well as the collective dreams of others who look up to you, remember your beginning and end, and that will ensure that you endure.

# WHAT DOES THE BIBLE SAY ABOUT ENDURANCE?

"Blessed is the man who remains steadfast under trial for when he has stood the test, he will receive the crown of life which God has promised to those who love him." —James 1:12

The above quote isn't just some abstract metaphor shrouded in mysticism that you need to use your extrapolation and imagination to make sense of. It offers some extremely practical and real advice about standing tall in the face of adversity that's valid and relevant even in today's world.

This sentiment is widely shared by almost all of the major religions of the world. Be it the Christian way of enduring through tough times with the help of your faith in God or the Buddhist way of facing all the troubles in life with calmness and serenity, all religions have advised this to their followers.

When you think about it, many saints and even Jesus Christ himself suffered through tough times in their quest for the righteous way. Adverse conditions have always tried to break down their spirit and faith in God but endurance kept them going through all difficulties and hardships.

Malcolm X said, "If you stand for nothing, you will fall for anything." That's very closely related to the idea of enduring tough situations and taking a stand for yourself. It's usually very easy to quit and take the easy way out, but convincing yourself to stay in the game, even when you feel like you're going to lose, takes conviction in yourself and your abilities and the strength of character to not lose that faith in the face of difficulties.

So, in tough times, you can always look to religion, even if you're not religious. Most religious texts have distilled millennia of human experience into a single book and you can find solace and advice there that will guide you on your journey.

# HOW GANDHI DEFEATED THE BRITISH

I'm sure you've heard of Gandhi. Mohandas Karamchand Gandhi was a barrister who had been trained in England. Soon after returning to his own country, India, he took up the cause of India's freedom from colonial rule and became one of the leaders of the Indian National Movement.

The one thing that separated him from other revolutionaries like George Washington was his insistence on nonviolence. He never resorted to any means of violence in anyway and, many times, gave himself up willing for arrest at the hands of the colonial police force. He was even beaten many times, but he never retaliated. He had garnered such a following in the first few years that if he had given the word, the entire nation would have taken up arms against the British. Instead, he picked the path of the slow burn. He protested peacefully against the British, simply standing outside their offices and police stations with huge crowds and doing nothing except standing there.

He even broke the laws that he felt were unfair. For example, there was a law that taxed salt in the country, much like the law taxing tea in the colonial America. Instead of pouring salt into the sea, he walked 200 miles to a place where salt was made, made some salt, and then gave himself up for arrest. The act not only gathered a lot of publicity but also made the UK look bad in the eyes of the rest of world. Soon enough, the law was repealed and Gandhi was freed.

And this pattern continued! He protested against many other unjust and draconian laws. He faced many difficulties too. He was beaten by the police in his protests, jailed, detained, and he fasted, but he endured it all. As a result, when the British left the country, they left it for good and at the terms of the Indians. On top of that, he was named the Father of The Nation and, to this day, every currency note in the country bears his photograph on it.

Gandhi's story has been one that has inspired many leaders from Nelson Mandela to Martin Luther King Jr. His example of endurance inspired much of the Civil Rights movement in the United States in the 1950s and 1960s. And that was how a single man, armed with nothing but a walking stick, managed not to only defeat the greatest empire in the world but also embarrass and humiliate it on the international forum.

*Considering the fact that I was stuck about business ideas, I started looking around for an internship. I was a man possessed. I had failed miserably and I had nothing more to lose. Which is why this was the time when I got the most done. I called other entrepreneurs and investors and ask to meet with them in order to understand what was they did and how they succeed at it. Many would reject me, a few rather rudely too, but I was adamant. I had understood that if I had to succeed, I couldn't wing it anymore. I had to know exactly what I was doing.*

*During one of these calls, I got in touch with my eventual mentor, Vevek. He had been an entrepreneur working on information products for the past few years and chalked up quite a following in the Internet Marketing circles. I was instantly attracted to this idea. It was a perfect business model for me to work on. Due to my extensive reading and experience in web design and content, I could work on this easily. It didn't require a lot of upfront capital, and all I needed to give was my knowledge and expertise in a particular topic.*

*I met with Vevek and, over the course of a few hours, decided that I wanted to work for him as an intern. He wasn't looking for someone else to join his team, but I convinced him to take me on as an intern. I even decided to forgo pay just so that I could stay in his team and watch him work and learn. Possibly, he saw some potential in me and decided that it was worth a shot. So he took me on. The next nine months were what I consider my Golden period, and, in more ways than one, shaped the entrepreneur that I am today.*

*However, despite it being the Golden period of my career and where I learned and grew the most, it was also the hardest part of my life. I was literally broke. I didn't have a nickel in my pocket and I couldn't pay for a bus ride to get to my job. Some days, I didn't have enough money to get a meal and stayed hungry for a day or two at a time. On top of that, during that time, my brother also joined me, as he was going to a college in the city. So I had to support him as well. I endured 80-90-hour work weeks with no days off. But all these trials and tribulations would soon payoff.*

*I devoted all the dedication and hard work I could muster in my internship for the next nine months, while holding a second job to pay my bills. I was still in debt and, even with two jobs, I wasn't making much headway into paying that off. After the paying the instalments of those, I sometimes I had less than $100 to last me a month. It was laughable, but I still hung in there, somehow. There were times when people told me to quit my internship and start looking for a real job, something that would help me pay off my debts, but I knew that all the time I was putting into my internship was an investment that would pay itself off many times over very soon.*

# RATIONALE

**RATIONALE**

*After working at the internship for nine months, I decided that I had learned enough to dip my toes into the pond, so I quit the unpaid internship and started working on my first digital product launch. I had been offered a full-time paid position by my mentor, which would have definitely eased things over. I would have had a steady income coming in. I had paid off most of my debt. I had been managing most of the work at my mentor's enterprise anyway, so I knew my job. Nevertheless, I decided to strike out on my own.*

*The thing with Rationality is that, for most people, it's often very difficult to separate the rational from the emotional. Many people would have thought that the rational thing for me would have been to take the job and take it easy for a while. I had paid my dues and my talent was finally being recognized and most people would consider throwing that away stupid. But that wasn't what I had set out to do. There were two reasons that convinced me of the rationality of my decision.*

1. *I had set out to be an entrepreneur. I couldn't be an entrepreneur while working for someone else. It went against what I had started to do (something we'll talk about in the Bonus Chapter at the end of the book). So, I wasn't going to make that compromise.*

2. *I had learned everything that I possibly could from the job to such an extent that I was now getting comfortable there. The job wasn't pushing me to my limits or challenging me anymore. I knew the problems that would come up, how to tackle them, how to deal with clients, and everything else. In short, I had accomplished everything I had set out to accomplish from taking this internship and gaining knowledge.*

*So, I decided to quit and started working on my first book. I worked really hard on the content and layout, taking care of everything on my own, almost micromanaging everything. I published it on the Amazon Kindle store and at the end of the first month, my first ever royalty payment came in. It was $13.*

*You might think that was a pittance. It actually wasn't. I would be below the poverty line if that were the only money coming in. But I was jumping on the bed. It was literally the first time I had made any money from business after dropping out of college. Those $13* *were the first sign from God that I could do this and now things were going to turn around.*

*This was where my story takes a turn for the better. My first book caught on. Not as well as I had hoped it would, but I started getting a few hundred dollars every month. Remember that I wasn't doing anything anymore. My job with writing the book was done. Except an occasional boost on Facebook or something similarly small, I wasn't doing anything major, but I was still getting passive income to the tune of a few hundred dollars a month (something that would later become the foundation of my business: Authority on Demand).*

*However, as I went deeper into the business, I noticed something else. People were earning way much more than I was even though our products were similar. I realized that I was missing something, but I wasn't quite sure what it was. I had to figure it out, but, this time, due to my previous experience, instead of trying a hit-and-miss approach, I decided to call in some expert help.*

*Looking around on the Internet, I came across my other eventual mentor, Gaurab Borah. He had been working with Digital Product launches and was one of the stars in that community. He taught a course offering his insights and other tips and tricks of the trade but it was way out of my budget. I would have been back to having a blank bank balance if I had paid his fee, as it would wipe out all of my savings.*

*Here, I had another choice to make. I could have gone on the way I was going and tried to figure everything out on my own by trial and error, or I could get some help and save some time at the cost of my savings.*

*It was a difficult decision to make, but, all this time, the industry had taught me to override my emotions and take decisions that would make sense rationally, even five years in the future. I knew Gaurab's reputation was well-earned and what he had to teach me wasn't some rehashed crap that I could find with a simple Google search. I decided to look at the whole deal as an investment rather than a cost. Keeping this in my head, I decided to go ahead with the deal and signed up for his course. It was a rational choice again. It sure wiped my bank account clean, but I knew that, in the long run, this investment would pay for itself many times over.*

*Once again, I threw myself into whatever he had to teach me. I completed his course, saw him work on his products and then, I spent the next few months playing around with what he had told me, tweaking his principles and ideas to find out the best combination for my particular products and books. Soon enough, much sooner than it would have taken me to figure out the system on my own, my book became an Amazon bestseller!*

*Rationale is an often left-out ingredient in a lot of books about entrepreneurship. Most people assume that it's common sense, but the problem is that many people, in the throes of emotion, confuse rational decisions with emotional decisions. A very good metric to judge the rationality of your decisions is whether those decisions make sense a few months after you've made them. If they don't, maybe you didn't make the best decision and should keep it in mind not to make the same mistake again the next time you're making a similar decision.*

*Rationale also keeps you on the track. Once you're sure that you've made a rational decision, you can be sure that you did everything you could, given the information that you had. If there are problems later on, you don't need to blame yourself and you can simply move on solving the problem instead of losing sleep over why you made that decision and blaming yourself.*

Adolf Hitler was depicted as a ruthless villainous character all over the world. Well, who doesn't know Hitler? He was probably the prime reason for the Second World War. He carried out the biggest invasion of all times on Russia and almost conquered it. Hitler turned the world upside down.

Many believe that he was an outstanding leader, motivator, and speaker. People stood mesmerized when he spoke. He had everything to convince the German population.

But still, we all know what became of him.

And can you see why?

Let me take you to another scenario and then we'll discuss how not to be like him.

There are many citations to what I'm about to say in the editorials of the world level newspapers.

Some members of many terrorist organizations are well-read teachers, doctors, engineers, software developers, and hackers who, if they wanted to, could help strengthen international security but don't.

Why? When they have so much extraordinary talent to help

the world, why do they choose terrorism over humanitarianism?

The answer is simple. They lacked something.

Although they had a Vision, Passion, Optimism, Willpower, and Endurance, they didn't have even a sense of Rationale and that's why they turned to destruction instead of development. These rationale-lacking leaders are, in fact, destructive leaders. Rationale is true reason; it's not rationalizing. Any terrorist or criminal can easily rationalize what they do, but that doesn't mean they consider it with sober, cold logic and reason.

Rationale is the water that pacifies the thirst of a vision. It doesn't let passion go haywire.

It's a moral value that rides optimism and willpower while giving a direction to endurance.

And the aura of rationale doesn't end there. You ought to use all the rationale you have but also all that you can borrow too.

A person without any rationale doesn't care about client satisfaction or about his customers for that matter. They don't want to satisfy their customers but only long for money and only money. They don't give a fish about where the money comes from.

If you're unfair with a single team member, then you give rise to a whole new series of negative thoughts in the other team members. They suspect that if one member can be treated that way, they could be too.

But, when a leader is in a committed relationship with rationale, he or she not only makes the team stronger but also brings in the necessary trust, which, in turn, inspires every individual of the team to deliver the best they can to every client.

# HOW NOT TO BE LIKE HITLER

I'll be able to explain Rationale better with this model. Let's get going and talk about a completely different scenario through this model.

A review of the pros and cons of the rational decision-making approach raises the question of whether such a model is actually a "rational" choice. While this model allows for taking structured and informed decisions, it places serious limitations that sap the vitality of an organization.

The rational decision-making model is a structured and sequential approach to decision-making aimed at seeking precise solutions to well-defined problems using precise methods. The decision maker derives the necessary information by observation, statistical analysis, or modelling and makes a systematic analysis of such "hard" quantitative data to choose from the various alternative courses of actions.

The rational approach to decisions is based on scientifically obtained data that allow informed decision-making, reducing the chances of errors, distortions, assumptions, guesswork, subjectivity, and all major causes of poor or inequitable judgments. Such an information- and knowledge-based approach promotes consistent and high-quality decisions that reduces the risk and uncertainties associated with decisions

The rational method infuses the decision-making process with discipline, consistency, and logic. It's a step-by-step approach that requires defining the problem, identifying the weighing and decision criteria, listing the various alternatives, deliberating on the present and future consequences of each alternative, and rating each alternative on the criterion. Such a sequential approach allows the decision maker to arrive at the optimal decision and refrain from becoming like Hitler.

The methodology caters to addressing complex issues by breaking it down into simple steps and considering all aspects of the problem with all possible solutions before making a final decision.

Among the steps of making a decision, evaluating the alternative solutions is crucial in the process of making a good decision. A good decision is determined not only by the experience and skills of the decision maker but also on the adequacy and validity of the information obtained from the different business environments. The information can be knowledge we already know or data that can be analyzed to derive some helpful and useful facts.

For example, from the data obtained from the sales for last year, a decision make can predict the sales trend and profit that might happen in this year to help make the promotion budget. Decisions are better when they're based on facts, educated opinions and logical reasons. So, the rational decision-making model can be used to make good decisions which might have the most desirable results.

To ensure that the decision made is the best, it must be rational. That is to say, the decision has to be based on reasonable data, facts, and reasons. So, rational decision making can be defined as "a systematic process of defining problems, evaluating decision alternatives and selecting the best alternative decisions available." The goal of rational decision making is to choose the best solution that will maximize the benefits and minimize any costs. There are some steps that decision makers can follow to make rational decisions.

# WHAT IS THE 7-STEP GUIDE TO RATIONAL DECISION MAKING?

**Step 1: Defining Problems:**

The first step of rational decision making is to identify or clarify the problem that needs to be addressed or solved.

**Step 2: Considering the goals:**

After the issue is identified, the decision maker should think about and determine the desired result or goal that he or she would like to achieve.

**Step 3: Developing alternative solutions:**

The decision maker should look for as many alternatives as possible for solving the problem. The more alternatives that can be generated, the greater the chance that the best solution can be found.

### Step 4: Evaluating/Analyzing the alternatives:

Each of the alternative solutions should be carefully evaluated according to its pros and cons. While evaluating, a lot of information should be collected first. Since the goals and desired results have already set in the above step, every alternative should be compared to see whether the optimal result could be reached with minimum costs. We get this information by observation, statistics, surveys, etc.

### Step 5: Selecting the best solution:

Based on the evaluations, the next step is to select the best alternative solution available. The chosen solution is called the decision. The decision should be the alternative that best fulfils the requirements.

### Step 6: Implement the decision:

Once the decision is made, the decision maker should put the decision into action, which means to implement it. Every stakeholder should be informed; sometimes, they're also involved in the decision-making process.

### Step 7: Evaluate the decision:

The last step is to evaluate the result of the decision to see whether the decision is good enough and appropriately addresses the problem. Also, some data and feedbacks from this decision can help in making decisions on similar problems.

Rational decision making brings a structured or reasonable thought process to the act of deciding. The choice to decide rationally makes it possible to support the decision maker by making the knowledge involved with the choice open and specific. This can be very important when making high-value decisions that can benefit from the help of tools, processes, or the knowledge of experts.

## WHAT DO YOU NEED TO STAY IN THE GAME FOR THE LONG TERM?

Decision making will follow a process or orderly path from problem to solution. Solving a problem isn't always by intuition or insight. In most cases, it's about sheer perseverance. In the same way you develop your passion, you need to grapple with a problem on a daily basis until you've solved it, instead of waiting for a Eureka moment. That process will give you many insights that you can use in your professional and personal life.

There's a single best or optimal outcome. Rational decisions seek to optimize or maximize utility. It might be time-consuming and difficult to get the solution exactly right, but once you do, you'll be a step ahead of your competition and be able to get the best clients and businesses to your doorstep with their requirements.

The rational choice will satisfy conditions of logical consistency and deductive completeness. Some things are true universally. One plus one equals two, without exceptions. Similarly, the decisions you make logically won't be falsified over time, assuming, of course, that you haven't left out important factors in your considerations.

Future consequences are considered for each decision alternative. This will be extremely important when trying to figure out the best solution. More often than not, the one solution that has the least negative consequences in the long run is the most logical one.

Risk and uncertainty are addressed with mathematically sound approaches. This is a relatively new approach but one that has been used with resounding success. Numbers don't lie and, as long as your research methodology isn't flawed, the results you get from this would be perfect and correct, as they're calculated by mathematical methods.

## HOW CAN YOU MANAGE YOUR TEAM SO THAT THEY CAN TRUST YOU?

I've been managing a team of ten people for over a year now and they trust me and my vision blindly because I like to keep every one of them on the same ground and play fair. Moreover, because they know that they'll never be treated unfairly, they try to put in their 100% as if it were their own venture. This was possible just because of the rational team management in our company culture.

On the basis of good decision making, a strong trustworthy team can be managed. The team will then do a great amount of things that we'll discuss further, but first, let's hear another story.

*A philosophy professor stood before his class with some items on the table in front of him. When the class began, wordlessly, he picked up a very large and empty mayonnaise jar and proceeded to fill it with rocks, about two inches in diameter.*

*He then asked the students if the jar was full. They agreed that it was. So the professor then picked up a box of pebbles and poured them into the jar. He shook the jar lightly. The pebbles, of course, rolled into the open areas between the rocks.*

*He then asked the students again if the jar was full. They agreed it was.*

*The professor picked up a box of sand and poured it into the jar. Of course, the sand filled up the remaining open areas of the jar.*

*He then asked once more time if the jar was full. The students responded with a unanimous "Yes."*

*"Now," said the professor, "I want you to recognize that this jar represents your life. The rocks represent the important things, such as your family, partner, health, and children, things that would make your life full, even if everything else was lost and only they remained. The pebbles are the other things that matter, like your job, your house, your car. The sand is everything else, the small stuff.*

*"If you put the sand into the jar first," he continued, "there's no room for the pebbles or the rocks. The same applies to your life. If you spend all your time and energy on the small stuff, you'll never have room for the things that are important to you. Pay attention*

*to the things that are critical to your happiness.*

*"Play with your children. Take your partner out for dancing. There will always be time to go to work, clean the house, give a dinner party, or fix the disposal.*

*"Take care of the rocks first, the things that really matter. Set your priorities. The rest is just sand."*

Here, there are many lessons to be learned from this story but the one we're focusing on is how to utilize time and resources for our greatest benefit.

A team can be managed at once, which will accomplish the following:

**Better Utilization of Resources:**

Decision making helps one to utilize the available resources to achieving the objectives of the organization. The available resources are the Six M's: Members, Money, Materials, Machines, Methods and Markets. The manager has to make correct decisions for all the Six M's, as they will result in better utilization of these resources.

**Facing Problems and Challenges:**

Decision making helps the organization to face and tackle new problems and challenges. Quick and correct decisions help to solve problems and to accept new challenges.

**Business Growth:**

Quick and correct decision making results in better utilization of the resources. It helps the organization face new problems and challenges. It also helps to achieve its objectives. All these result in quick business growth. However, wrong, slow, or no decisions can result in losses and industrial sickness.

### Achieving Objectives:

Rational decisions help the organization to achieve all its objectives quickly. This is because rational decisions are made after analyzing and evaluating all the alternatives.

### Increases Efficiency:

Rational decisions help to increase efficiency. Efficiency is the relationship between returns and cost. If the returns are high and the cost is low, then there's efficiency and vice versa. Rational decisions result in higher returns at low cost.

### Facilitate Innovation:

Rational decisions facilitate innovation. This is because it helps to develop new ideas, new products, new process, etc. This results to innovation. Innovation gives a competitive advantage to the organization.

### Motivates Employees:

The rational decision results in motivation for the employees. This is because the employees are motivated to implement rational decisions. When the rational decisions are implemented, the organization makes high profits. Therefore, it can give financial and nonfinancial benefits to the employees.

**Problems and limitations with choosing rationally:**

Most of the issues and limitations associated with a rational choice result from falling short of the ideal prescribed in the full rational decision-making model. Here are three areas that generate much of the concern.

Limits of human capabilities:

The limits on our human ability to gather, process, and understand all the information needed to optimize a decision outcome makes it impractical to meet the ideal except in very constrained or simple situations. We have limits on our ability to formulate as well as solve very complex problems. Our desire to optimize is also limited and we'll usually "sacrifice" or compromise with acceptable solutions when faced with obstacles.

**Limits on information and knowledge:**

The model assumes we should or can gather sufficient information on quantity, quality, accuracy, and integrity. It also assumes that we have access to the required knowledge of the cause and effect relationships that are important to the evaluation of alternative solutions, particularly with respect to projecting future consequences.

**Limits in time:**

Searching for the optimum solution will generate a delay that could negatively impact the benefits of the chosen alternative. In essence, if the decision alternatives aren't properly discounted for changes due to decision timing, the chosen alternative may not be optimum.

*I wrote one more book and published it on Amazon. I applied some promotional strategies and my second book became a bestseller. During the next month of my publishing, I made $448 from my books. I was really confident about self-publishing because I got the clear picture of how to write and publish a book and make it a bestselling.*

*Rationale can be the most powerful tool in your arsenal in letting you decide what to do and how to take your business further. This has been my strategy ever since I started. Sure, it's difficult at times to decide whether a decision is truly rational or not but that's something you get only once you've jumped into the arena. You could dissect every decision you could have made from the sidelines but that would mean nothing when compared to hard, cold, real-world experience you gain yourself.*

*So, after I had written a couple of successful book and had ensured a steady passive income, I started looking at my greater responsibility as an entrepreneur. I realized that there must be several people all over the world who had unique skills and knowledge and experiences to share but couldn't do so because they didn't know how to. Think about it, what if you could learn woodworking and carpentry from someone who had built a career making wooden furniture or you could learn music from a musician who had been playing live for decades. Wouldn't it be exciting to get not only knowledge but also inside scoops and insights accumulated from years of experience?*

*So, to address this need, I created an information product on how to write and publish book and used my savings to launch it on an international platform. As expected, it was a huge success. Thousands of people bought the product. Of course, I made money out of it, but I was happy because I was able to contribute to society and help people not only realize their dreams of telling their stories but also enabling millions of people to read life stories that would have gone unsaid otherwise.*

*I was able to show people the right path of becoming a successful indie-author. It was possible just because of the Rational Decision. I could have hogged that knowledge and turned out book after book, but the respect, satisfaction, and recognition that info product brought me was worth more than whatever money I could have earned.*

*Humans are capable of developing into rational beings. This is our ultimate assumption. At some level, all of us want to effectively analyze and solve our problems. We want to live significant and meaningful lives. We want to be persons of integrity. We didn't consciously choose to be selfish and egocentric, any more than we consciously chose to think unclearly, inaccurately, irrelevantly, superficially, narrow-mindedly, or illogically. BUT, we often think and behave egocentrically. We often think unclearly, inaccurately, irrelevantly, superficially, narrow-mindedly, and illogically.*

*Rationality often not only affects you positively but also contributes to the society. Go back to Adam Smith, the father of modern Economics. He claimed that in a society of rational people, everyone working for their personal good helps the common good as well. That was exactly my objective.*

*Now, I had open several stream of income through online. Now, I was an entrepreneur. I was making money through books, through product launches, through email marketing. I learned several skills, from creating a website to writing content to creating videos, and, you know what, everything is sellable.*

*I made money though all my skills. Finally, I was a winner. Now, the people who doubted me at first were saying, "I knew you would make something out of your life." It was hilarious watching them change their tune overnight. I thought again and found out that leaving the rat race of being an engineer and following my passion of being an entrepreneur was a rational decision. I was happy. My parents were proud of me.*

*I cannot emphasize this enough. The best metric to judge a decision's rationality is whether it make sense a few months after you've made it. If not, maybe you didn't make the best decision. Remember that so you don't make the same mistake again.*

*I desired to start a company with a difference. So I started Authority on Demand, which helps experts, entrepreneurs, and coaches to establish their authority by helping them become a bestselling author. In Authority on Demand, we provide all the services related to publishing with my team of around fifteen people. I applied the rational decision in my daily life in this company. And those decisions have, so far, helped the company to grow exactly the way I had envisioned it to. This brings us to the last*

# NUCLEUS OF THE P.O.W.E.R.
# STAR VISION

*"Where there is no vision, the people perish: but he that keepeth the law, happy is he." —Prov. 29:18*

In this chapter, we'll talk about the nucleus of the P.O.W.E.R. Star, Vision and, necessarily, about

**"What's your BIG WHY?"**

Your why is different from your passion in that it's the big picture behind your passion. For example, the person who edited this book has a passion for editing and ghostwriting self-help books, but his BIG WHY is to help aspiring self-help authors leave a written legacy of their wisdom and life experiences for other to benefit from.

What is your BIG WHY? Is it reviving the education of your country because you see children begging on the streets when they should be in school?

Is it living life on your own terms that don't enslave you?

How about seeing that smile on your parents' face?

Or maybe seeing yourself at a position so strong that you don't have to think twice to purchase anything whatsoever?

There is a different Why for every person on the planet What's yours?

About that, let me tell you a very small story which includes a maid, an innocent orphaned child and how they became an inseparable part of my life and yes, how they gave me the vision of life and made me into who I am now.

*This happened shortly after I had dropped out of college and was working on my first business.*

*I had hired a maid who used to cook for me.*

*One day, circumstances were such that I had to pay a visit to her house.*

*I was just about to leave when I saw a child of about five or seven who was doing the dishes. When I looked closely, I saw that he looked occasionally out of the corner of his eye at other children who were playing marbles.*

*Even when he finished doing the dishes, he just watched other children play and enjoy themselves.*

*I became interested in this child and, out of sheer curiosity, asked him, "Why don't you go and join them?"*

*To which he said, "I can't play with them. They speak in English sometimes, and then I feel out of place."*

*So my obvious question was, "Don't you go to school?"*

*To which he replied with a succinct "No."*

*He became sad and further added, "I can't afford to go to school. I have to work to earn my daily bread."*

*I read sadness all over his face and tried to cheer him up by smiling and said, "Do you want to study?"*

*There are some moments in our lives when a person doesn't even utter a single word yet makes the other person entirely understand what one was supposed to give words to.*

*This was one of my moments.*

*This child didn't say anything at all but I could behold the sparkle in his eyes when I asked him if he wanted to study.*

*I left, for if I'd stayed even a few seconds longer, tears would start rolling from my eyes.*

*But I can still clearly see those sparkling innocent little eyes.*

*Later that day, I came to know that this child was an orphan. He was left with my maid by her cousin's sister so that the child, being in a big city like Delhi, could at least make a proper living.*

*As I heard this, my heart sank. I was shattered.*

*I said to myself. Oh! Irony! You tiny piece of junk!*

*Here, I am, who just left studies in the middle of a course, whatever the reason may be, and there lives a child with twinkling eyes, who works day and night, washing dishes to just survive, who doesn't even know whether he would have a meal tonight or sleep on an empty stomach. But still, he badly wants to study and to play with other children with his head held high.*

*I asked myself what use would money be if I couldn't bring happiness to such a zealous would-be citizen of my country. And, at that exact moment, I pledged that I'd dream and innovate but I would also fight to empower such enthusiasm and support the vulnerable in every way possible.*

*Sometimes, when I fail even after working very hard, I get frustrated with everything and just want to quit.*

*But you know what? Those sparkling innocent little eyes don't let me quit. They get me started every time. Every time, I begin again with this vision of mine of why I had begun in the first place.*

*And I redoubled my effort with even greater zeal to work for that little soul.*

My actions may not always bring happiness but there would be no happiness without those actions. The actions decide the purpose of your life, which becomes important as you get older. This is especially true when a person matures from imitating their heroes and mentors.

As Oprah stated in an interview, she realized that she could be a much better Oprah instead of trying to be a Barbara Walters. When we reach this point, we focus more on having a vision for our lives.

A vision is essential to having a positive outcome and it's vital to success. Learning new things is great for the brain and will create new pathways of thought and focus.

When centered and applied properly, a vision will allow one to gain new insights and abilities to create not only a new way of life but also a new world around them. A vision is a picture or an idea one may have in the mind for self, business, or any other future endeavour.

Clarity of that vision helps you to pursue dreams, achieve goals, and produce a more successful and prosperous outcome. A clear vision will open your mind to endless possibilities and unlimited points in the future. Having a vision is one of the most important factors in the path of your success in life.

You feel much more valuable as a person when you set and

achieve visions and goals. When visions and goals are set and defined, the value of the person is increased exponentially.

# HOW TO CREATE YOUR VISION IN 4 SIMPLE STEPS?

Let me sum it up for you on how to create your vision in four simple but yet appealing steps. You will have to read between the lines to comprehend it completely.

Yet again, I'm providing you with a step-by-step manual to create your Vision. Here are the four steps that you need to follow:

Step 1. Do what you love. Oh yeah! Just pursue what you're really into. Why waste your life or time or your talent for that matter, for anything that you don't wish to do. When you do what you love to do, you at least come up with something original instead of the artificiality that's present at almost every corner.

Step 2. Think Big. Don't let small incidents change the direction of your way of living and steer you clear off the road to miraculous success. Have big goals and think even bigger.

Step 3.  Be Specific. Absolute necessity! We all know, more or less, what we desire to achieve in our lives. That's good, but good isn't good enough here. You also need to know what you don't desire, and then you'll be specific about everything in your life.

Step 4.  Start Taking Action. Your vision may be hazy when you first look at it, but when you start taking actions, it becomes clearer and clearer. Don't sit in front of a log, expecting a lightning bolt to strike it. That may be how the first campfire started. But cave dwellers used their ingenuity and initiative to find other ways of lighting fires. So light you own fire. There's no mercy in this competitive market, but, as long as you keep taking actions, you'll survive. You'll survive better than anyone else has before.

## WHY DO YOU NEED TO START WITH A VISION?

The answer is simple. Without a clear and precise vision of exactly what you desire, you'll never reach it or have it. The more clearly focused you are on exactly what you desire, the easier and faster you'll manifest everything you need to make it a physical reality. Since all material things move from the nonphysical to the physical reality, your vision and goals are paramount in the process of achievement. Your vision and focus acts like a magnet that attracts and connects the pieces together. When you focus on what you truly desire rather than what you think you want or what others say you should want, you engage your heart, your feelings. And this gives you added energy and creativity to manifest your desire.

*A vision is the capacity to see beyond your current reality, creating and inventing what doesn't now exist and becoming what you are not right now.*

A vision is important in all aspects of life: physical, mental, and emotional. When you have a vision, you can overcome obstacles in the way and hold on when times are tough. A vision that's well defined helps you to focus and create a purpose that becomes the measure of your success.

*A vision will open up your mind to many possibilities and a brighter and bigger future.* When you can envision a future that's better, happier, and more productive, you're more likely to make the changes you need to reach that type of life. The destination of your vision should be emotional, physical, spiritual, and intellectual.

Having a vision established is an essential key to success during your path through life. It establishes whether you win or lose in regards to how, when, where and what you receive and possess. By achieving visions and goals, humans feel valuable, showing the potential of their inner self. Having a vision is very spiritual.

The process of connecting with your vision is intricate. You'll see with your mind and soul and not with your physical eyes. There will be moments when what you see with your physical eyes contradicts the entire vision.

## HOW CAN YOU USE THE LAW OF ATTRACTION TO FUEL YOUR VISION?

The law of attraction is the name given to the maxim "like attracts like", which in New Thought philosophy is used to sum up the idea that by focusing on positive or negative thoughts, a person brings positive or negative experiences into their life. This is Wikipedia's definition of the law of attraction.

This is equally true in our scenario as it is in any other. So, when you start thinking positive about your Vision, believe that it's already manifest.

You need to wish and then intend, which will equip you with the prerequisite to receive. This prerequisite fuels your Vision to wish for more and intend to achieve it even better.

Start by loving your Vision and your life and see how they'll love you right back.

Make a mental picture of what you desire in your mind, add feelings of joy and gratitude to that mental picture, see yourself taking every step to its completion, give thanks in advance as though you've already received it, and keep the emotions congruent with the vision. When you do that, your vision will come to fruition and manifest something beyond your wildest dreams. Having a vision demands persistence and discipline.

In order to become a successful entrepreneur, you must first have vision. Visionary entrepreneurs have the ability to see today as it is and calculate a future that grows and improves. A successful entrepreneur can see the future and still stay focused in the present.

For a successful entrepreneur, a vision isn't seen as a dream but a reality that hasn't quite come into existence. For entrepreneurs, a vision is easily perceived because their levels of dedication and confidence stand strong. Entrepreneurs are able to spend hours upon hours to bring their visions into reality. Their vision acts as a force within them, driving them to action.

In order to establish that type of drive and vision, YOU need to know exactly what you want. Ask yourself where you want to see yourself in so many years. Do you want to be healthy? Wealthy? Tell yourself specifically how you picture your life. Anything is possible within a vision.

When you build your vision, think big. When you create a successful vision, you begin to feel passionate about it. The only way to be successful in your vision is to visualize it and set goals and a plan of action to reach your vision.

Over time, you'll begin to see more parts of your vision coming true until one day you see yourself living it. Building your vision doesn't have to be difficult as long as you know exactly what you see for yourself in the future. Your vision should include who you want to be. It's important to know clearly who you are right now in order to know who you want to become. This includes your habits, attitudes and points of view. If you're not clear about yourself, you won't be clear about your future. Choose your vision wisely and precisely. Precision is key. You are unique. There may be many people who share your general vision, but only you have a specific, unique version of it that no one else has. When you find that niche with a defined vision, riches beyond your imagination in every area of your life will be yours!

## WHAT HAPPENS IF YOU GO ON WITHOUT A VISION?

If you don't have a vision of who you want to be, how you want to succeed, or what you want out of life, you begin to lack drive and your life becomes just an order of events. A strong and current vision connects with your passion and greatest potentials. Regardless of what's going on in the world or challenges that present themselves, a vision helps you know what you're doing and why you're doing it.

Once, a man went to a fisherman and asked: "Why are you sitting *at the shore during the day if you could be going out fishing?"*

*"I've caught enough fish and I don't need any more,"* the fisherman replied.

*"Well, if you went out fishing, then you could catch more fish and sell those you don't need in the marketplace,"* the man explained.

*"Why would I need to do that?"* the fisherman asked.

*"Then you could get money to buy more boats and catch more fish and be able to make even more money!" explained the man.*

*"And why would that be good for me?" enquired the fisherman.*

*The man said, "Well, then you would eventually have enough money to hire other fishermen to do the work for you, and thus, you wouldn't have to work so much and you would be able to rest during the day."*

*And the fisherman replied: "That's exactly what I'm doing right now."*

The story of the fisherman shows that it might be much easier for you to get the essence of what you desire to have, instead of getting the things that you believe would bring you the core of what you want. Simply stated: to have the freedom to do anything you'd like to do, doesn't require ten million dollars in the bank, but you'd have to work on a lifestyle business, so you could do it anywhere in the world or in the comfort of your own home.

In order to feel more loved and cared for and get rid of a sense of loneliness, you wouldn't necessarily need a new relationship, but you would have to start loving and taking care of yourself more, and being happy to spend time on your own.

In order to feel better about the way you look, you wouldn't necessarily need to be in perfect shape, but you would have to love yourself exactly the way you are and to ignore the ridiculous expectations that society has about people's looks.

If you're able to get the essence of what you desire in the first place, then the things you would like to have in the physical world would flow into your life more easily as well.

So, if you start working on a lifestyle business and are free to do it anywhere in the world, then probably, you'd eventually begin to make lots of money as well.

If you love and take care of yourself and feel happy being with yourself, then it's much easier to attract a partner like that as well.

If you're already happy with the way you look, then you won't feel the need to lose weight in order for people to like you more, and thus, be able to much more easily achieve your dream body shape without having any additional pressure to get there.

## WHY WOULD YOU FAIL IN LIFE?

Failure can mean different things to different people. For some, it might be something as small as not landing that dream job. For others, it might be something as lofty as not being remembered by everyone once they're dead. People are all motivated by different things and what works for one person may not work for another.

One tragedy of modern times is that everyone's definition of success has become identical. Think about it. When would you call yourself successful? When you have a big house, a nice car, some money in the bank, a happy family? This was the definition of success back in the 1960s, and, sadly, people of all cultural backgrounds have accepted that definition. However, it doesn't have to be that way. We need to realize that, as individuals, success can mean different things for different people, and that's perfectly fine. No one success is more valid than others.

In the same way, failure can also mean different things to different people, and even that is perfectly permissible. After all, when people's definitions of success are unique to their personalities, why shouldn't their failures be too?

But herein lies the million dollar question. How do you know what failure is for you? How do you separate your unique definition of failure from what the culturally accepted definition of failure is and try your best not to fail according to your metrics?

This is where you need to have vision. When you have vision, you're extremely clear about what you've set out to do. Once you have knowledge of that, it would be extremely easy for you to figure out what the opposite of that, failure, would be for you.

For example, for me, money, a big house, etc. are all secondary. My primary vision has been all along to help as many people as possible to live a life that they desire to have with freedom, both financial and emotional. Thus, I gave away all my insights to the rest of the world when I could have hogged them and made a fortune. But that had never been my vision. I firmly believe that the money you make is direct proportional to the number of people you help, and, for me, helping other people has always been more important than merely accumulating wealth.

So, take some time out every day and think about what you desire to do with your life. Figure out what your successes and failures are. Once you've figured that out, stick with them and work accordingly to fulfil your personal vision without getting distracted by everyone around you. Their definitions of success are different from yours, and that's perfectly fine. You cannot compete with them because they're playing by their rules, not yours. An added bonus is that once you realize the difference in the definitions of success for people and stop comparing yourself to them, you cut out a lot of stress from your daily life, which will go a long way toward making your life happier and more peaceful.

This is how you can avoid failing in life, by knowing exactly what your failure is and working hard to move in the opposite direction.

## HOW CAN YOU FIND YOUR PURPOSE INSTANTLY?

Define everything from your likes and dislikes biggest fear and mistakes to the greatest adventure you've ever had. The key word here is Define. As you define the essence of what you desire your life to look like, you complete the first and most important step toward manifesting your dreams into reality.

Every big accomplishment in the world started from someone's vision. By creating a very clear and precise vision of your own life, focusing on the essence that you're looking for, you set the stage for it to eventually become true.

Start now by paying attention to what you're good at and like doing. Listen to the compliments others give you about what you do well. Keep a list of these skills and qualities to become conscious of and to excel at these talents. Your excellence, achieving your goals, and becoming aware of your unique skills leads to the vision of your life.

Your vision will then propel you to the stratosphere of an extraordinary life experience that contributes to the world while fulfilling your purpose.

So, with all that's been said and defined as the importance of having a vision as an essential part of your life, YOU need to water YOUR VISION seed daily.

In the light of the above, I highly recommend that you take at least fifteen minutes of your day to picture in your mind your vision and feel it so that you can outpicture it in your life. You may not be a CEO yet, for example, but you can talk, walk, and act like one. Just as an acorn contains the potential to be a mighty oak tree, so do you contain the potential in your Vision seed to become a CEO or whatever your purpose is.

Water that seed daily and you'll see its manifestation. You provide the seed, the universe provides the resources. Therefore, you must now make your "new vision" inside your brain more real than the current reality in your outside world. But that's only half of cultivating your purpose. The other half is purposeful action based on the vision. That's the fertilizer that will transform your vision from a tiny seed to a full-grown tree that bears fruit. Then and only then will the universe begin to present its riches to you and your vision will become a reality.

*"Vision without action is merely a dream; Action without vision just passes the time. Vision with action can change the world."*
—Joel Barker

The following story illustrates the difference between just having a job and having the power of Vision. It's a story about three bricklayers, but it could be the story of three mail clerks or three CEOs.

*The story goes that three bricklayers were working side by side.*

*A passerby who was curious about what they were building asked, "What are you doing?"*

*The first bricklayer replied: "Can't you see? I'm laying bricks."*

*The second bricklayer was asked the same question. He answered, "I'm earning money to feed my family."*

*The third bricklayer, when asked the question, replied, "I'm building a cathedral."*

*The question you need to ask yourself is, "Am I trying to reach my goals in my business as a bricklayer or as a cathedral builder?*

In this regard, I want to tell another story, a true story about an 80-year-old man, which shows that it's never too late to find your vision and fulfil your purpose. The story is taken from a speech by Joe Plumeri at the 2014 Venture Atlanta conference of the Technology Association of Georgia.

*About 24 years ago, an 80-year-old man from Trenton, New Jersey had a vision to rebuild his community. He had been there all his life, and, at the time, Trenton wasn't fairing too well. The economy was depressed and people were moving elsewhere to look for work.*

*One day, this 80 year old man started talking to his son, Joe Plumeri. He told his son he had a vision where he revitalized Trenton by building a baseball stadium. His father spoke with such clear vision and passion that Joe told him that if he got the city to approve and zone the stadium, Joe himself would buy the stadium and a team. A year later, the city approved the stadium.*

*How did this 80-year-old man get a stadium approved in one year? Joe's father handed out fliers, spoke passionately to others about his vision, and organized a 1,500-person candle march to City Hall. Through his passion and determination, he raised enough money, to bring a minor league baseball team to town. He envisioned building a better community that would attract and keep people. This 80-year-old man with a clear vision, brought over $20 million a year to the city, and has showcased the Minor League Team of the Year for 5 of the last 23 years.*

I share this story because, as you face your business challenges and you think your obstacles are too hard to overcome, think about this story. Think about how this 80-year-old-man organized all of this with no technology, no formal knowledge of baseball or stadium construction. He only had a clear vision and a determined passion to change his community.

What are the challenges standing in the way of your vision? What is the vision you have passion behind? What cathedral or stadium are you destined to build?

Once you clearly identify the vision for your life, you'll work tirelessly to manifest it.

# THE SWAN SONG
## THE LAST-MINUTE
# P.O.W.E.R

**"The only way to do great work is to love what you do. If you haven't found it yet, keep looking. Don't settle." —Steve Jobs**

I wrote this book to show that everyone has the right to succeed. The potential to become a successful entrepreneur is in your own hands.

Life isn't, and never will be about sitting in a cave and meditating to discover your true self; it's all about activating your true self. You just need to pursue your strengths, and success is sure to follow.

You must always keep in mind that no matter how long the journey, it always starts with a single step and that single step determines the direction and course of the journey.

*"A frog decided to reach the top of a tree and all the other frogs shouted that it's impossible. Still the frog reached the top, how?*

*This was because he was mostly deaf and he thought all the shouting was to encourage him!"*

You have the patience, strength, and passion to achieve your ambitions, goals and dreams. All you need to do now is TRY (To Realize Yourself).

You know all those things you've always wanted to do?

*You should go do them, now.*

*And you'll ask will it be easy? Nope. Worth it? Absolutely! Because at first, they'll ask why you're doing it. But later, they'll ask how you did it.*

So, just go. Work hard in silence and let success make the noise.

To summarize, I'd like to say that anyone can become successful and fulfilled in her/his own field, and, for that, we just need to remember and apply the P.O.W.E.R. star.

Wherever you deal with people, you can readily apply P.O.W.E.R. and get results from that moment on. Make a wish and intend to achieve it and you'll find the whole universe conspiring to let you achieve it!

Explore.

Dream.

Create.

# IN A NUTSHELL

*"The whole secret of a successful life is to find out what is one's destiny to do, and then do it." —Henry Ford*

**Find your destiny and enjoy success** by following the simple rules of the P.O.W.E.R. Star:

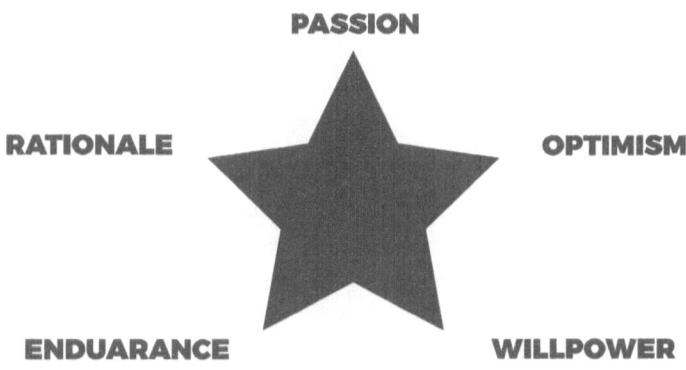

## P- PASSION

Success comes to those who dedicate everything to their passion in life. You can do anything as long as you have the passion, the drive, the focus, and the support.

## O- OPTIMISM

Optimism is the faith that leads to achievement. Pessimism leads to weakness while optimism leads to power. So, instill optimism in your thoughts, act accordingly, and you'll achieve your goal.

## W- WILLP.O.W.E.R.

Willpower is the key to success. "It is fatal to enter any war without the will to win it." So, it's important to have the will to succeed and then no one can stop you from reaching your goal.

## E- ENDURANCE

If Passion is what gets you started, then endurance is what keeps you going. No great entrepreneur has ever walked this planet who didn't have the ability to endure hardships and difficult situations. If you desire to be successful in anyway whatsoever, you need to be able to endure difficulties.

## R- RATIONALE

Immanuel Kant wrote, "All our knowledge begins with the senses, proceeds then to the understanding, and ends with reason. There is nothing higher than reason." A genuine quality of a leader is the ability to take the right/rational/logical decision in a given situation.

## V- VISION

This holds the most important and highest position of the P.O.W.E.R. Star- the CENTER. Roy T. Bennet said, "Great leaders *create more leaders. Good leaders have vision and inspire others to help them turn vision into reality. Great leaders create more leaders, not followers. Great leaders have vision, share vision, and inspire others to create their own.... Live the life of your dreams: be brave enough to live the life of your dreams according to your vision and purpose instead of the expectations and opinions of others.... Create a vision for the life you really want and then work relentlessly towards making it a reality."* Without VISION, an entrepreneur is nothing; because entrepreneurship is the capacity to translate vision into reality.

# ABOUT THE AUTHOR!

Vikrant Shaurya is a creative and compassionate twenty-four-year-old individual who made his way to glory with the help of his perseverance.

He is known for helping people launch their books and making them bestsellers on Amazon so that they can build their authority in their industry. His life's goal is all about moving forward and taking as many people as possible along with him. That's why he started "Authority on Demand" through which he would help you tell your story to the world and help you get recognition and create your own brand in this noisy and boisterous marketplace.

He's helped a lot of people around the globe become bestselling authors and create a passive income empire for themselves. Vikrant is a motivational speaker and a man of action!

With more than four successful five-figure information product launches and a #1 bestseller book under his belt, Vikrant Shaurya is definitely a fast evolving entrepreneur.

Vikrant loves intelligent conversations and engages in meditation to soothe his mind and body.

To find out more, just say Hi. Please hop in for a marvelous journey to the better you!


www.vikrantshaurya.com